THE STEWARD'S TOOLBOX

THE STEWARD'S TOOLBOX
Skills and Strategies for Winning at Work

Edited by Mischa Gaus

A LABOR NOTES BOOK

A LABOR NOTES BOOK

Copyright © 2012 by Labor Education and Research Project

About the publisher:

Labor Notes is a monthly magazine of labor news and analysis intended to help activists put the movement back in the labor movement. It is published by the Labor Education and Research Project, which holds a biennial conference for all labor activists, acts as a resource center, and puts on schools and workshops on a variety of topics. Visit our website at www.labornotes.org.

Reprints:

Permission is granted to workplace activists, unions, rank-and-file union groups and labor studies programs to reprint sections of this book for free distribution. Please let Labor Notes know of such use, at business@labornotes.org, 313-842-6262, or 7435 Michigan Ave., Detroit, MI 48210. Requests for permission to reprint for other purposes should be directed to Labor Notes.

Cover Design: Stacey Luce

Inside Design: Jenny Brown

ISBN-13: 978-0-914093-00-8

CONTENTS

Acknowledgments   xi

Introduction   1

ONE   STEWARD SKILLS

Handling Insubordination Grievances   5
   David Cohen

Understanding and Defending Past Practices   9
   David Cohen

Proving Disparate Treatment to Win Discipline Grievances   13
   Robert M. Schwartz

Confronting Blame-the-Worker Safety Programs   17
   Nancy Lessin

Representing Members at Investigatory Interviews   21
   Robert M. Schwartz and Clark Peters

Defending Workers against Discipline   25
   Robert M. Schwartz

Defend Your Breaks, and Defeat Retaliation   29
   Ellen David Friedman

Action on the Job: Tips and Traps   33
   David Cohen and Judy Atkins

Turning an Issue into a Campaign   37
Ellen David Friedman

When Bad Gripes Happen to Good Stewards   41
Ellen David Friedman

TWO   BARGAINING

Mid-Contract Concessions: What to Do?   47
Richard de Vries

Bargaining Tactics for Pensions   51
David Cohen

Bargaining for Health Insurance   55
Peter Knowlton

Bargain to Organize, Organize to Bargain   59
Matt Luskin

Make Technology Work for Us, Not against Us   63
Charley Richardson

Just Say 'No' to Drug Tests—Then Bargain   67
David Cohen

THREE   RUNNING FOR OFFICE, RUNNING THE LOCAL

Building a Team to Win Local Union Office   73
William Johnson and Dan Lutz

Election Flyers that Win Votes   77
William Johnson and Dan Lutz

Laying the Groundwork Before You Run   81
Chris Kutalik

Avoiding the Missteps New Officers Make   85
Dan Campbell

FOUR COMMUNICATING WITH MEMBERS AND THE PUBLIC

Winning the P.R. War in a Contract Campaign   91
    Randy Robinson

Boost Organizing with Social Media   95
    Paul Abowd

When Your Boss Doesn't 'Like' You: Surviving in Social Media   99
    Mischa Gaus

Using the Airwaves to Educate and Mobilize Workers   103
    Tiffany Ten Eyck

Putting Labor Films to Work   107
    Chris Garlock and Jon Garlock

FIVE ORGANIZING FROM THE BOTTOM UP

Building a Stewards Council   113
    Paul Krehbiel

A Strong Stewards Council Can Win a Big Campaign   117
    Paul Krehbiel

How to Break Down Craft Divisions through a Campaign   121
    Paul Krehbiel

How to Involve Young Members   125
    Tiffany Ten Eyck

Defeating Privatization   127
    David Cohen

Home-based Workers Create a New Kind of Steward   131
    Hetty Rosenstein

Losing Dues Check-off and Thriving   135
    David Cohen

Surviving without Check-Off   137
   Tom Smith

Under Right-to-Work Laws: Organizing under the Gun   139
   Paul Ortiz

Stewards Committee Jump-Starts Action across Unions   143
   Bill Franks, Ron Blascoe, and Barbara Smith

SIX — DEFENDING EVERYONE

Let's Talk Immigration in the Union   149
   Tiffany Ten Eyck

Immigrant Defense Action Networks   153
   Jerry Mead-Lucero

Protecting Lesbian, Gay, and Transgender Members   157
   Donna Cartwright

Making Sure All Families Benefit   161
   Julie Robert and Helen Ho

Constituency Caucuses Can Speak to Many Needs   165
   Guillermo Perez

Winning Sick Leave at the Citywide Level   169
   Young Workers United

SEVEN — COALITION-BUILDING

What a Lasting Union-Community Alliance Looks Like   175
   Jeff Crosby

Public Employees Fight to Save Services and Jobs   179
   Carol Lambiase

Building a Coalition from the Grassroots to Fight Cuts   183
   Howard Ryan

Find Allies, Not Just Supporters   187
   Greg Asbed and Lucas Benitez

L.A. Teachers Use Privatization Fight to Build Community Power   191
   Noah Lippe-Klein and Sherlett Newbill

Getting Members Involved in Occupy's Next Phase   195
   Joe Berry and Helena Worthen

EIGHT STRIKES AND CONTRACT CAMPAIGNS

How UE Members Occupied Their Plant   201
   Leah Fried

Preparing for, and Winning, a Public Sector Strike   205
   John Braxton and Karen Schermerhorn

Sympathy Strikes and the Law: Is Solidarity Legal?   209
   Robert M. Schwartz

Striking Back against Picket Line Retaliation   213
   David Cohen

Reviving a Lost Art: Building a Strike Support Committee   217
   Chris Kutalik

Everything You Were Afraid to Ask about Lockouts   221
   Robert M. Schwartz

How We Built a Caucus and Won a Great Contract   225
   James Fouts, Scott Ranney, and Chuck Norris-Brown

Taking a Contract Campaign Public   229
   Carol Lambiase

CONTRIBUTORS   233

ACKNOWLEDGMENTS

The Steward's Toolbox is the product of years of month-by-month effort by scores of union activists, staff, and leaders committed to building our movement from the grassroots.

They are the unsung heroes of the labor movement. They share their expertise without reward, or even adequate thanks, as we *Labor Notes* editors rush from story to story. They step back from the crush of daily tasks to analyze and evaluate, and then teach the rest of us.

Seeing their combined effort of five years brought into a collected whole should remind us of the enormous experience that rank-and-file activists can draw on. I find reassurance during these dark days in the knowledge that we have so many seasoned leaders ready and willing to train the next generation.

I'll single out a few: Dave Cohen, Bob Schwartz, Ellen David Friedman, Paul Krehbiel, and Charley Richardson have been mainstays, each adding several irreplaceable contributions to *The Steward's Toolbox*.

Labor Notes couldn't produce its books, or our monthly magazine and daily website, without folks like these. You can read more about them on page 233.

I offer my deepest gratitude to the Labor Notes staff, especially Jane Slaughter and Jenny Brown. Jane shepherded the original form of many of these articles into print. She has been a force for democratic unionism and precise writing. Jenny designed and produced the book, improved the editing, and has been a thoroughly patient and thoughtful collaborator. Thanks too to Mark Brenner for his consistently sharp pointers, to Chris Kutalik and William Johnson for their years guiding *Labor Notes*, to Stacey Luce for her excellent cover design, and to Jim West, Mike Konopacki, and Slobodan Dimitrov for generously permitting us to use their photography and cartoons.

Every book is a shared project but this one especially so.

Mischa Gaus
Editor, *Labor Notes*

INTRODUCTION

If the union movement is going to find its way back from the wilderness, it will depend on new leaders.

Where will we find them? Shop floor activists are the raw material for labor's revival.

From grievers to strike captains, labor's best leaders for more than three generations have come from among the ranks of the stewards. They are the people seasoned by the fight.

Our movement needs thousands more stewards with the skills, confidence, and authority to stand up.

But the steward must have a bigger perspective. They push back against management not just to defend members but to balance the scales more broadly.

They know the power of the union is rooted in our ability to stand up to the boss where we work. They see the union as an instrument to help us chart a future for ourselves, to gain a sense of control over our work.

If that promise is to be kept, members need to see the union come alive. This book lays out many of the essential skills stewards and leaders need to make the union a credible threat to management's power.

WITH A LITTLE HELP

These 55 articles first appeared in our monthly magazine *Labor Notes,* mostly in the Steward's Corner column.

Much training for stewards focuses simply on grievances. Our authors have gone much further, looking at how to win in many arenas and with many tactics.

For one thing, we can't win the big fights on our own. Alliances with the community, ties to faith groups, students, parents, and the users of the services we provide, all of these help us win.

But they also make the union stronger. Linking up with others can help show that labor believes its responsibilities extend to all people. Labor is not a "special interest," and we can prove it by joining with partners to say the community's needs and the workers' needs are wrapped up in one another.

Working in coalition with other groups is tough for many unions. Partner groups might not operate under the same pressures as the union, nor do they have the same resources.

But the rewards can be significant. The unions we profile fought off budget cuts, saved schools from privatization, and kept people in foreclosure from losing their homes.

Part of that battle is getting the word out. But when "union" has practically turned into a dirty word in the media, how can labor tell its side of the story? Hiring slick PR firms and paying consultants to "craft our message"—people can smell the fakery a mile away.

We included examples where unions harnessed both the new media and the old, training our most persuasive storytellers—rank-and-file members—to share the union's perspective.

With bargaining rights under assault, and outrageous concessions demanded everywhere, strong internal organization is more important than ever. Creating stewards councils, hand-collecting dues when check-off disappears, and linking the political assault to our organizing has helped some unions survive—and even thrive—in a difficult environment.

Finally, we learn from unions that didn't take labor's best weapon, the strike, off the table. They dusted off strategies that once made labor strong, even a factory occupation.

It's not the easy path. But there are no shortcuts on the road to rebuilding union power.

GO DEEPER WITH LABOR NOTES

For much more on organizing on the job and off of it, see *A Troublemaker's Handbook 2*, a 372-page manual for workers who want to take control over their lives at work. In hundreds of first-person accounts, workers tell how to run all sorts of campaigns, from a march on the boss to a contract campaign to an organizing drive. It's the most thorough handbook on the market.

Democracy Is Power is the handbook for running a strong union. Learn how to get members to participate, how to plan a good union meeting, how to run a fair election, what to do when you first take office, and how to lead when you're not in office, too.

To order see store.labornotes.org. Get both books for just $30.

Chapter One

STEWARD SKILLS

HANDLING INSUBORDINATION GRIEVANCES

by David Cohen

Ella was having a bad day. Her machines weren't running right, but her foreman came over and said, "Ella, we need those machines up and running, and since Rafael is out today, I want you to start up his machines, too."

"No way," said Ella. "I've got my hands full, and the contract says I don't have to run extra machines except in emergencies."

"I'm telling you to get over there and start up those machines," yelled her foreman. "If you don't, you'll be fired for insubordination."

Sally, the department steward, went to the supervisor's office. "We have to talk about your foreman," she said. "He's threatening Ella and trying to make her run more machines than she's supposed to."

Benito shot back, "I'm the one who told him to get Ella off her butt. I don't have time now, talk to me tomorrow."

"We're going to talk about this now," Sally said.

"Oh yeah?" snarled Benito, "Get out of my office or I'll have you fired for insubordination, too."

Management loves power. Threatening to punish workers for insubordination is a handy tool for reinforcing a supervisor's power on the job.

For union people, the idea of punishing workers for being "insubordinate" to bosses—that is, uppity— is insulting. The concept reveals the anti-worker bias of labor law: management is considered the "master" and workers are considered "servants" who should show proper respect.

WHAT IS INSUBORDINATION?

Here is one management description: Insubordination is a deliberate and inexcusable refusal to obey a reasonable order that relates to

> **Employees have the right to question and argue with the boss, within limits.**

an employee's job. Employees may not decide for themselves which instructions they will follow and which they will not.

This is how most arbitrators or the National Labor Relations Board (NLRB) would describe insubordination. But there are different levels, and management's behavior often has an impact on whether the worker's actions are considered insubordinate.

There are two basic tests: Was the worker given a clear, direct order? Did the worker clearly know the consequences of refusing the direct order? This usually means the supervisor must tell the workers what will happen if they refuse.

This does not mean the boss can immediately give a worker a direct order with the threat of punishment and not have to listen to objections. Employees have the right to question and argue about an order.

WHAT IT ISN'T

It is not insubordination if a worker asks questions or gives reasons why he or she shouldn't have to do the assignment.

It is not insubordination if the worker asks to have a steward explain to management how the order violates the contract.

It is not insubordination if following the direct order will immediately put someone's life in danger. The threat, however, has to be real and immediate.

It is not usually insubordination if the supervisor giving the order is not the worker's normal boss or part of the "chain of command" that the worker ordinarily has to follow. Workers should insist on finding the regular supervisor and asking that person to make the decision as to what they should be doing.

It may become insubordination if the worker consistently refuses after being directly ordered to perform the task.

It may be insubordination if the worker does not argue but then never carries out the order.

NOT IN FRONT OF THE KIDS

Here's another example of class bias: arbitrators look at whether the supposed insubordination takes place in front of other workers. They tend to rule more harshly if the "master" is ridiculed or disobeyed in front of other "servants." In some cases arbitrators have ruled against workers when they bragged about what they told the boss in private.

"Shop talk"—the use of salty language—is not automatically insubordination. Look at the context: How much shop talk goes on regularly? Do supervisors use it? Do supervisors and workers ordinarily use it with each other?

Many workers have been cleared when it was shown that management harassed them and they responded with a poor choice of words. Still, a worker may be considered insubordinate for using excessive shop talk after being told to do something.

What should a worker do if following an order will cause damage to a machine, produce a poor product, or result in inferior services for the customer? Clearly point out what the bad results will be and ask for a witness to that warning. A worker who does this generally cannot be disciplined for the resulting damage.

STEWARDS' SPECIAL STATUS

NLRB rulings have given stewards a special status in regard to insubordination, saying, "When stewards are engaged in representational activities they are considered equals with management."

This means that when stewards are dealing with management as a steward, they can engage in robust disagreement, can use profanity to some extent, and generally do not have to show deference. Stewards have a right to vigorously pursue an argument with management.

As the NLRB said in one decision, "the relationship at a grievance meeting is not a 'master-servant' relationship but a relationship between company advocates on one side and union advocates on the other side, engaged as equal opposing parties."

WHAT ABOUT ELLA AND SALLY?

Ella's situation is a classic case of harassment, but she needs to be careful. She was given a direct order and was told what would happen if she refused. But Ella has a right to argue her case, and the boss jumped the gun by threatening her right away.

Sally the steward is within her rights to stay in the boss's office and continue arguing the case. Benito is running afoul of labor law, because a steward cannot be threatened for doing her duty to represent workers.

Sally is in a grievance situation, and Benito cannot just dismiss her and refuse to talk.

UNDERSTANDING AND DEFENDING PAST PRACTICES

by David Cohen

Stewards need to know what the past practices in their workplace are—to defend them from erosion by management.

A past practice is any longstanding, frequent practice that is accepted and known by both union and management. A *bona fide* past practice is considered part of the contract, so grievances can be filed if management violates a past practice. *Be sure to check your contract for any language that may limit the use of past practices for grievances.*

In most cases management cannot end a past practice without first bargaining with the union. In some cases management must wait until contract negotiations to change a past practice.

The union can enforce some informal understandings—even when not clearly in the contract.

There are three categories:

• **Contract-clarifying past practice,** the strongest type. When contract language is vague or general, the practice clarifies the general language. For instance: Contract language reads, "The company will allow union stewards *reasonable* time off to attend union meetings." For many years the company has allowed stewards to attend monthly union meetings and three times a year the district council meeting. This practice now clarifies and backs up what the contract means by "reasonable."

With such a strong past practice, an employer must bargain to change it and cannot change it if the union doesn't agree.

• **Independent past practice,** not addressed by any contract language. Most often these are "benefits" that workers take for granted and so were not included in the contract.

For instance, perhaps in your shop there have always been vending machines in the cafeteria and free parking in the company lot. Management cannot just do away with these benefits.

Management can terminate independent past practices under three conditions:

1. It can prove the original conditions that started the practice have changed significantly.
2. It can prove significant ongoing employee abuse of the practice.
3. It notifies the union during contract negotiations that it will end the practice during the next contract.

Even in the first two situations, the employer must bargain with the union before ending the practice.

Most arbitrators will not extend these past practice rights to work methods.

For instance, if management wants workers to run three machines instead of two, claiming new technology makes them easier to run, the union probably cannot claim it is a past practice that workers run only two machines. However, the union can demand that management bargain over a change in working conditions.

- **Contract-conflicting past practice.** These are the hardest to prove, with most arbitrators saying the contract should prevail. However, the arbitrator may rule in favor of practices that have existed for a very long time, happen very frequently, very clearly conflict with the contract, and were very clearly known to both parties.

Say that the employer has never given union reps absentee "points" for attending union conventions, even though there are no such provisions in the contract. This has been going on for 10 years, and the union notifies management each time as to who will be attending. In this case, although the practice conflicts with the contract, it probably would be considered valid.

The employer must notify the union of its intent to end this type of past practice and must bargain if the union requests. After bargaining, the employer may end the practice.

The tests for a valid past practice are:
- **Has existed for a reasonably long time.** The longer a practice has been in effect, the more weight it carries. Many arbitrators think that a practice must be three to five years old and must have been in practice during at least two contracts.
- **Occurs repeatedly,** the more times the better. A practice that happened a few times four years ago and hasn't happened since is not strong. An exception might occur around a holiday. If every year for

seven years management allows workers to go home early Christmas Eve, this could be a valid past practice.

- **Is clear and consistent,** repeated the same way each time. If there are minor deviations, there must be at least a predominant pattern of consistency.

An example might be around personal phone calls at work. Perhaps management has always let workers accept them, and the union can document more than 100 times in the last five years. If management points out three occasions where workers were refused the right, the overwhelming pattern is in favor of the union.

- **Must be known to both management and union.** While a past practice does not have to be "negotiated," it must be something that both parties know about. Sometimes it's not good enough for a low-level foreman to know; it must be higher management. In one shop workers left a little early on Fridays for years. According to the absentee program, they should have received one point, but the foreman never gave points for Friday. Upper management found out and decided to give everybody warnings.

The union could have argued against the warnings because management did not inform the union that it wanted to change the practice. However, since upper management did not know about this practice, it would be hard to win.

- **Must be accepted by both management and union.** Often the fact that a practice occurs frequently over a long period of time indicates that the parties agree to it. A practice that is openly agreed to by both parties gains past practice status more quickly than one that is not openly accepted. When management acknowledges a past practice as part of a grievance answer, its "legal" status is much more secure.

An example: For years, workers have been allowed to line up at the time clock after the first bell rings, signifying five minutes til quitting time. A new boss says no one can line up til the quitting bell rings. The union has a strong case: the fact that management never did anything to stop this practice indicates acceptance.

When filing a grievance, gather plenty of evidence on how long and how frequently the practice took place, and how the employer knew about it. The more, the better.

[This article is based on attorney Robert M. Schwartz's useful book, *How to Win Past Practice Grievances*. It can be ordered from Work Rights Press at www.workrightspress.com.]

PROVING DISPARATE TREATMENT TO WIN DISCIPLINE GRIEVANCES

by Robert M. Schwartz

Claiming "disparate treatment"—imposing harsher punishment on one employee than was imposed on others who committed the same offense—is one of the most effective union defenses against discipline, especially discharges.

Careful research of the employer's records can ensure members are treated fairly.

When disparate treatment is proven in arbitration, discipline must be either vacated or reduced.

Although company training manuals invariably warn management against disparate treatment, the practice is hard to root out. Some bosses enjoy dispensing favors to brown-nosers, personal friends, or workers who inform on the union. Others are too lazy to make sure discipline is consistent.

Some examples of disparate treatment:

- Suspending worker A for speeding while giving no punishment to worker B
- Firing worker A for fighting while allowing worker B to enter into a last-chance agreement
- Firing worker A after a single warning, while giving worker B two warnings before termination
- Firing worker A for absenteeism while allowing other substance-abusing employees to enter treatment programs

In a case flawed by disparate treatment, the proper remedy is to reduce the penalty to the level imposed on the lesser-punished worker or workers.

It may seem easy to establish disparate treatment: simply request a raft of disciplinary records and search for employees who violated the same rule or standard as the grievant but were given lesser punishment. Yet unions who pursue such cases often find their claims rejected because the union is unable to counter the employer's contention that the differences were justified.

UNDERSTANDING THE RULE

Contrary to common assumption, the disparate treatment rule does not require an employer to treat all employees alike. Harsher discipline can be imposed if there is a legitimate reason.

For example, the grievant may have a substantially worse disciplinary record, may have committed a far more serious infraction, or may have substantially less seniority. Employees may get lenient treatment if they admit their mistakes or take responsibility for their actions.

To prove disparate treatment, the union must fully research the comparison employees, studying their personnel files, reviewing their investigatory interviews, and, most importantly, talking with them about what happened. (In many cases, these employees must be called to the stand.)

Even the records of fired workers should be reviewed: the union may discover that a fired worker was given two warnings before the final action, while the grievant received only one.

GRIEVANCE SETTLEMENTS

Workers often receive less punishment than others as the result of a grievance settlement. For example, the employer may agree to reduce a discharge to a suspension or a suspension to a written warning. If the union cites these cases at arbitration, will they be accepted for comparison purposes?

It depends on the language. If the settlement says that it is "without precedent for future cases," or uses words to this effect, it will have no value before an arbitrator (although it may be raised in the lower steps of the grievance process). If, however, the settlement is silent on precedent, the arbitrator can classify it as disparate treatment.

Q&A

HOW FAR BACK CAN WE GO?
Q. Can the union go back 10 years to prove disparate treatment?

A. Yes. In one published case an arbitrator ordered reinstatement because the employer issued a lesser penalty 14 years earlier.

NO DIVERGING PENALTIES
Q. A short-term employee was terminated for an offense that a long-term employee was given a warning for. Is this legitimate?

A. No. Although a difference in seniority can justify a discharge over a suspension, it does not justify such a wide divergence of penalties.

DIFFERENT DEPARTMENT
Q. Can an employer justify harsher discipline for insubordination on the ground that a lesser-punished employee works in a different department?

A. No.

HOW MANY EXAMPLES ARE NEEDED?
Q. Do we need several cases to prove disparate treatment?

A. Although more is always better, most arbitrators will find disparate treatment from a single example.

SUPERVISORY MISCONDUCT
Q. Does the disparate treatment rule apply to infractions by supervisors?

A. Yes, if the supervisor (or other non-bargaining unit employee) violated the same rule as the grievant and was not punished and if the rule applies both within and outside of the bargaining unit (such as a no-smoking or no-fighting rule).

UNION REPRESENTATIVE
Q. Can an employer take harsher action for a violation because the employee is a steward?

A. No. Union representatives cannot be held to higher standards of conduct than rank-and-file employees except in areas, such as wildcat strikes, where the contract imposes special obligations on union officials.

PERMANENT BAR?

Q. If an employer suspends a worker for sleeping on the job, is he permanently barred from discharging others for such violations?

A. No. Prior treatment disappears as a defense if the employer notifies the bargaining unit that in the future all employees who commit the offense will be discharged, with no consideration of mitigating circumstances.

CONFRONTING BLAME-THE-WORKER SAFETY PROGRAMS

by Nancy Lessin

In a Missouri food warehouse, 150 workers load and unload trucks, lift boxes, drive fork trucks, and move endless pallets. Each month that no one reports an injury, all workers receive prizes, such as $50 gift certificates. If someone reports an injury, no prizes are given that month.

Last year, management added a new element to this "safety incentive" program: if a worker reported an injury, not only would co-workers forgo monthly prizes but the injured worker had to wear a fluorescent orange vest for a week. The vest identified the worker as a safety problem, and told co-workers who had lost them their prizes.

The myth is that injuries result from bad behavior rather than hazardous conditions.

Employers' approach to health and safety is often to blame workers themselves. They claim injured workers weren't using the equipment properly, or they weren't paying attention. But what is seldom asked is—why?

For decades, employers have brought in work-restructuring programs such as Lean, Six Sigma, and *kaizen*/continuous improvement. The result was understaffing, work overload, long hours, job combinations, and too few workers doing too much work—and therefore increased stress, repetitive strain, and other injuries and illnesses.

Increased injury rates brought higher workers compensation premiums and meant a higher risk of OSHA inspections. Supervisors lost bonuses, and facilities faced the loss of safety awards that had helped them win investments and contracts.

But instead of rethinking their work restructuring, employers came up with a different plan: hide the injuries. Enter "behavior-based safety."

KNOW THE ENEMY

These programs and practices focus on worker behavior rather than on workplace hazards as the cause of injuries and illnesses. They include:

- Safety incentive programs, where workers receive prizes or rewards when they *don't* report work-related injuries
- Injury discipline policies, where workers are threatened with or receive discipline (including termination) when they *do* report injuries
- Post-injury drug testing, where workers are automatically drug-tested when they report an injury
- Workplace signs that track the number of hours or days without a lost-time or recordable injury, which encourages numbers games
- Other posters, such as those stuck to washroom mirrors stating, "You are looking at the person most responsible for your safety."
- Behavioral safety observation programs, where workers observe co-workers and record their "safe behaviors" or "unsafe acts." These programs focus attention away from hazards and reinforce the myth that injuries result from bad behavior rather than hazardous conditions.

HIDING HAZARDS

In order for there to be a workplace injury or illness, there must be a *hazard*. A union approach to reducing injuries and illnesses is to identify, eliminate, reduce, and prevent hazards. A behavior-based approach, on the other hand, drives both injury reporting and hazard reporting underground. When a job injury or illness is reported, the hazard causing it can be identified and addressed. If injuries aren't reported, hazards go unaddressed—and injured workers may not get the care they need.

In addition, if a worker is trained to observe and identify fellow workers' "unsafe acts," he or she will report "you're not lifting properly" rather than "the job needs to be redesigned."

It's hard enough to get hazards fixed that we know about; it's impossible to fix hazards we don't know about.

Many behavioral safety programs also harm union solidarity by pitting worker against worker. When workers lose prizes if a co-worker reports an injury, peer pressure comes into play. When workers observe co-workers to record their behavior, solidarity suffers.

Employers tout low injury rates as an indicator of safety, when the reality can be disastrously different. One employer with a safety incentive program and an injury discipline policy won an award from the Massachusetts Safety Council for having zero recordable injuries. Minor injuries had occurred on a machine, but were never reported. The next year a worker was crushed to death in this machine.

Steelworker members inspecting safety logs.

Behavioral safety programs hide injuries, but they can't cover up fatalities. In 2005 BP was touting an OSHA injury rate many times below the national average at its Texas City facility, when an explosion there took the lives of 15 workers and injured another 180.

TAKING THEM ON

Whether employers use the carrot, the stick, or both, the results of such programs are the same: fewer workers report symptoms, injuries, and illnesses.

Unions need to educate members about the downsides of these programs. Incentive programs that promise prizes for not reporting injuries are hazards in disguise; observation programs are harmful even if they don't have discipline attached. Building solidarity around the need to end these programs is an important first step.

• Unions whose employers are covered by the NLRA or similar labor law should use their bargaining rights to block unilateral implementation of these programs, as health and safety is a mandatory subject of bargaining. See tinyurl.com/TroublemakersHandbook-h-s for a sample letter requesting to bargain and a sample letter requesting detailed information on the program.

• Unions whose employers are covered by OSHA can use a provision in OSHA's Recordkeeping Rule: it is an OSHA violation to discriminate against workers for exercising their right to report injuries. When workers lose prizes or receive automatic discipline for reporting injuries, this can be illegal discrimination under 29 CFR 1904.36 and Section 11(c) of the OSH Act.

One example was at Alcoa: the names of everyone who didn't report an injury went into a hat, and periodically there was a drawing for a big screen TV. Steelworkers Local 105 filed an OSHA complaint, and OSHA made Alcoa cease and desist.

In another case, an employer called in 17 members of USW Local 880 in Massachusetts and told them they had too many injuries—one more and they were up for termination. A call to OSHA produced a call to the company informing management that this was illegal discrimination.

MOBILIZE ACTION

Visible symbols like buttons and stickers demonstrate unity to management. At the Dunlop Tire plant in Alabama, management promised workers it would reward a low injury rate with a hot dog dinner during work hours. The union, USW Local 915L, explained to members that the actual goal was to discourage reporting. At the end of the time period, it happened that reported injuries had gone down, and the employer organized the dinner. The union organized a boycott. On the day of the picnic, out of 1,800 members, 1,798 refused to go. The union likes to say, "Management was eating hot dogs, hamburgers, and beans for a long time."

Unions can respond to the employer's signs announcing how long the workplace has gone without an injury with our own signs or leaflets that track how long it takes for the employer to address a particular hazard: "It's been 14 days since the union asked management to fix the slip hazard at the entrance, and they still haven't corrected it!"

Any checklist used in a behavioral observation program can be turned into its opposite: instead of recording co-workers' "unsafe acts," observers record only hazards: *"guard missing on Machine #3," "understaffing in the Emergency Department."*

At the food warehouse in Missouri, the members of USW Local 11-500 approved the purchase of fluorescent orange vests for every member. These vests would each bear the USW's sticker *"Fix the Hazards—Don't Blame the Victim."* Before this solidarity action was implemented, the employer "voluntarily" discontinued its orange-vest policy.

[For more information on confronting behavior-based safety programs, see www.hazards.org/bs.]

REPRESENTING MEMBERS AT INVESTIGATORY INTERVIEWS

by Robert M. Schwartz and Clark Peters

When management meets with a union member to ask questions about possible misconduct, the employee can request the presence of a union representative and refuse to answer until the rep arrives. These are known as *Weingarten rights* (from a 1975 Supreme Court case).

Weingarten rights apply to "investigatory" interviews, not to run-of-the-mill shop floor discussions. An employee who is unsure whether a conversation is investigatory should ask, "Could this meeting lead to discipline?" Unless the employer gives a firm no, the employee should request representation. The employee can select any available representative.

Stewards should use disciplinary meetings to prevent misrepresentations from entering the record.

Unless required by the contract, employers do not have to alert employees about their Weingarten rights.

The union's job at an investigatory interview is to (1) help the worker avoid making damaging admissions; (2) learn about the case; and (3) point out mitigating circumstances.

STEWARDS' RIGHTS

As a union representative, you have four rights at a Weingarten interview:

1. On arrival, you can request the reason behind the meeting, i.e., the rule or misconduct being investigated. The employer must cooperate. If your request is ignored or denied, instruct the employee not to answer any questions until the employer complies with its Weingarten obligations.

2. Upon being told the reason for the interview, you may ask for a private meeting with the employee. This is called a "caucus." The employer must give you adequate time and privacy.

3. When the interview resumes, you may raise objections to intimidating or confusing questions (but not to the point of blocking the interview). If the employee becomes rattled, ask for another private conference.

4. When the interview concludes, you must be permitted to cite extenuating circumstances that the employer should consider before imposing any discipline.

TIPS

Use the caucus to learn about the case and to explore possible defenses. Advise the employee not to act out, make insubordinate comments, or deny matters that are obvious (such as "Did you use your computer yesterday?"). Sometimes "I don't remember" is the best response.

Explain to the employee that guilt can be inferred from a failure to deny a charge. If the evidence is ironclad, the employee's best recourse may be to accept responsibility, apologize, and promise that the conduct will not be repeated.

Inform management that you wish to be present during any other interviews that are part of the investigation.

Take word-for-word notes of the interview.

Ask management for a chance to interview its witnesses.

MITIGATING CIRCUMSTANCES

When appropriate, at the end of the interview you should raise one or more of the following mitigating or extenuating circumstances:

SNAKES IN A TRUCK

If an employee has an innocent explanation for what appears to be misconduct, she should voice it at the Weingarten interview instead of waiting until a grievance meeting or an arbitration hearing. A worker who puts forward an account from the beginning is more likely to be believed.

In a famous published arbitration case, a truck driver testified that he crashed his truck because he saw a snake on the passenger seat, grabbed it with his hands to avoid being bitten, and attempted to steer with his knees.

Although the driver told this story from day one, he was fired for unsafe driving. Since there was no way for the employer to disprove the worker, and since the employer has the burden of proof, an arbitrator sustained a grievance protesting the worker's discharge.

- The employee's conduct was provoked by a supervisor or fellow employee.
- The company has not enforced the rule against other workers (a defense known as "lax enforcement").
- The employee was not properly trained on the job in question.
- Other employees have received low-level discipline, such as verbal warnings, for similar infractions.
- The employee has an excellent record or long service, is a good worker, has good attendance, and gets along well with fellow employees and supervisors.
- The employee suffers from a physical or mental condition, illness, or stress which may have affected his or her work or behavior.
- A supervisor's inattention or negligence contributed to the events.

WRITTEN STATEMENTS

Clark Peters, a veteran grievance handler for 1199NE/SEIU, adds the following advice on written statements:

Employers sometimes ask workers to review and sign notes taken by the investigator during the interview. Beware: Once the notes are signed, management can use them as the worker's written statement.

Before signing any notes, the worker and the union rep should read them carefully, pointing out any misrepresentations and insisting on any needed changes or additions. The union should ask for a copy and should advise the member ahead of time not to sign if the employer refuses.

A better alternative is to tell the employer that the worker would rather compose his or her own statement, with the union's assistance. Ask for time to prepare a complete account and insist on privacy. Bring a laptop so the union will be sure to have a copy.

Compose the statement in chronological order without extraneous information. Don't speculate, and keep it short. Go over the statement at least twice to make sure it is as accurate as possible.

If there is insufficient time to do a proper job, ask the employer for permission to turn the statement in later in the day or the day after.

DEFENDING WORKERS AGAINST DISCIPLINE

by Robert M. Schwartz

Knowing the guidelines for discipline and discharge cases is a critical skill for any steward or union rep. Here are some of the rules and theories that have emerged from recent arbitrations.

FORCED RESIGNATION

Q. Can we submit a grievance for a nurse's aide who resigned from work after her supervisor falsely accused her of patient abuse, threatened to discharge her, and suggested that she quit?

A. Yes. Under a theory called "constructive discharge," a resignation extracted by duress or coercion is considered equivalent to a discharge.

RETRACTING A RESIGNATION

Q. When a supervisor demoted a worker, the worker lost it and declared, "If that's how you feel about me, I quit." That night she called the union and said she had made a big mistake. Management says a quit is a quit. Can we grieve under the just cause standard?

A. Yes. An employee who quits her position because of emotional stress can retract the resignation if she gives prompt notice by telephone, fax, or email, and if the employer will suffer no significant harm by permitting the employee to return.

APPLYING RULES OFF-DUTY

Q. Does a work rule prohibiting the use, sale, or possession of controlled drugs apply when an employee is off-duty?

A. Generally, no. Company rules do not apply to off-duty conduct unless expressly stated. Even if the rule says it applies off-duty, the union can challenge the rule as unreasonable if the prohibited conduct does not have a demonstrably adverse impact on the workplace.

DRUG TEST

Q. A worker failed a drug test. Can the employer fire him without an interview?

A. No. Under due process principles, the employer must give the employee a chance to explain why he was taking the banned substance and why he should not be punished.

DOUBLE JEOPARDY

Q. An employee threatened another worker. Two hours later, his supervisor said, "If you do that again, you will be in a heap of trouble." The next day, human relations called the worker in and suspended him for a week. Can we defend on the grounds of double jeopardy?

A. Yes. A worker cannot be disciplined twice for the same conduct. The first notice was a verbal reprimand. The worker viewed it as final and continued working. The matter should have ended there.

ANONYMOUS COMPLAINT

Q. Personnel fired a driver after an anonymous customer sent a letter containing graphic descriptions of sexual misconduct. Do we have a chance at arbitration?

A. Yes. An employer cannot justify a discharge solely on the basis of hearsay. If the driver consistently denies the charges, and the complainant does not appear to testify, an arbitrator is likely to order reinstatement.

REASONABLE EXPLANATION

Q. A driver drove his truck into a guard rail. He claimed he saw a large snake on the passenger seat and grabbed it with both hands to avoid being bitten. Impossible case?

A. No. When a discharge is based on circumstantial evidence (no witnesses), the evidence must eliminate reasonable explanations advanced by the employee. If the driver gave the snake explanation from the get-go, and stayed with it consistently, he should prevail at arbitration.

LIE DETECTOR TEST

Q. An employee suspected of theft declined to take a polygraph test. Can the employer cite her refusal as evidence of guilt?

A. No. Arbitrators disfavor polygraph tests. They almost never hold refusals against employees.

DISPARATE TREATMENT

Q. The company discharged a five-year worker for sleeping on the job. Two years ago, a worker with 20 years' seniority was given a one-day suspension for the same offense. Does the difference in service time justify the difference in penalties?

A. No. Differences in seniority do not justify wide divergences in penalties.

DOG ATE IT

Q. Management says it lost the paperwork that explains why it issued a lenient penalty two years ago. Is this sufficient to avoid a finding of disparate treatment?

A. No. An employer cannot escape a finding of disparate treatment by asserting that paperwork has been lost or misplaced.

PICK YOUR POISON

Q. The company fired a worker who was seen smoking marijuana in her car. Six months earlier a worker who drank beer on the job was given a five-day suspension. Isn't this disparate treatment?

A. Yes. There is no acceptable basis for imposing substantially harsher penalties on employees who commit drug offenses than on employees who commit similar alcohol offenses.

ERASING DISPARATE TREATMENT

Q. If an employer suspends an employee for sleeping on the job, is it barred from firing future offenders?

A. No. An employer can erase past leniency by making a clear and unequivocal announcement to the workforce that it intends to discharge employees for all such offenses in the future.

PROGRESSIVE DISCIPLINE

Q. Our contract has a four-step progressive discipline policy. An employee with 20 years' service committed four offenses and was discharged. But in an earlier case, management gave a 22-year worker with four offenses another chance. Can we raise disparate treatment?

A. Yes. The employer surrendered its right to insist on a lockstep application of the progressive discipline provision. If mitigating circumstances are considered for one employee, they must be considered for all.

UNION STEWARD

Q. A union steward was punished for sloppy work. During a grievance meeting a supervisor said that she expected the steward "to set an example." Could this be enough for us to win the case?

A. Yes. Holding a steward to a higher standard of conduct than other workers violates the National Labor Relations Act as well as any contract provision forbidding discrimination against union officials.

ZERO TOLERANCE

Q. The company manual says any violations of safety policies "shall result in termination." Is this penalty binding in arbitration?

A. No. Arbitrators frequently rule that zero-tolerance policies are trumped by contractual just-cause clauses.

TO LEARN MORE

Bob Schwartz's new book is an in-depth look at just cause from the union perspective. *Just Cause: A Union Guide to Winning Discipline Cases* is packed with techniques, sample cases, and tips that will help you to make the best possible case for victims of unfair or excessive discipline. Published by Work Rights Press, it's available from store.labornotes.org.

DEFEND YOUR BREAKS, AND DEFEAT RETALIATION

by Ellen David Friedman

The economy is sour and job vacancies aren't being filled. Employees with seniority are being hounded into early retirement, with the result a de facto speed-up—new demands, heavier workload, extra responsibilities.

One day a younger worker comes to you, looking exhausted and pissed-off. He's had to absorb the workload of two other staff who've left and not been replaced.

He complains that he hasn't taken a coffee break or normal lunch for months. He shows you an "open letter" he's written naming the top executive as a greedy SOB and demanding that the work rules in the contract be honored. He wants to leaflet the whole workplace.

Inoculate folks against the retaliation that is sure to follow bold actions.

As a steward, you're happy to see someone willing to take action, rather than just complain. But on the other hand, you know that although this guy has the right to distribute a leaflet to his co-workers, his rights won't amount to much once he paints a target on his back.

EMBED AND PROTECT

In most workplaces these days, it is sensible to be scared of retaliation if you try to show any worker power. This is true even if you have a union, even if you have good contract language against retaliation, and even if your union has a good record of fighting the boss.

What to do, then? How do you resist relentless speed-up, fight to keep contractual breaks, and encourage the young worker in a way that builds support behind him and protects him when the inevitable retaliation comes?

Ask some questions that will help "embed" the problem he is having in a picture of the overall workplace.

Help him see that his problems are shared by lots of co-workers—and help him identify allies. Perhaps he should take his open letter around and ask for co-signers. Set a goal, a minimum number of signatures he should get, before he considers releasing it.

Make sure the number is high enough and broad enough—representing different work sites, job titles, and seniority levels—so that a clear message is sent to the employer that this is not an isolated gripe. And encourage him to include clear, concrete remedies. For example: restoration of regular breaks; a guarantee that lunch periods will be work-free; no new unilaterally assigned duties.

As the letter is being circulated for signatures, talk about what collective steps people can take to back it up with action. How about printing up small cards with the contract clause that guarantees break time, and handing the card to any supervisor who attempts to guilt-trip someone into skipping her break?

Could a big group all go on break at exactly the same time on one day, no matter what the work demands were? Would they be willing to walk through a worksite ringing a bell to announce break time? Theater and humor always help.

INOCULATE

At this stage it's necessary to "inoculate" folks against the retaliation that is sure to follow bold actions.

In one-on-one conversations, and eventually in leaflets and posters that can be distributed openly, explain ahead of time that retaliation is expected.

Spell out what it may look like—some individuals may be singled out for "performance review" or written up for trumped-up infractions. Others could be penalized with new assignments or given bad schedule changes, or find themselves the object of malicious gossip spread by boss loyalists. Someone could even be suspended or fired.

Name it openly to defuse the shame and fear that follow these sorts of attacks.

Describe the steps people should take if they become a target: First, the retaliation should be exposed by talking and writing about it.

Second, the facts should be mustered to build the case that this is retaliation for workplace activism.

Third, supporters should be ready to protect the victimized colleague with their own actions, such as petitions and pins (*You can't scare us!*) and, of course, through filing grievances and unfair labor practice charges.

Smart stewards analyze the power relations within the workplace, and identify and isolate any bosses who may be vulnerable. If a strong case can be made against a particular boss for his own bad behavior, upper-level executives may be willing to sacrifice that person to regain workplace peace.

Our labor history abounds with stories of workers taking action on behalf of a brave colleague who stood up and was smacked down by an employer—even wildcat strikes. These stories don't all end in victory, but they leave us with a legacy of purpose and self-respect that we can try to live up to.

ACTION ON THE JOB: TIPS AND TRAPS

by David Cohen and Judy Atkins

Workers have the right to organize and take action inside the workplace against an employer, even with a contract and grievance procedure in place. Section 7 of the National Labor Relations Act guarantees this right, but there are many restrictions.

Stewards and union reps need to be militant but smart. They need to know how to bend the rules without getting their people in trouble. Here are two examples of how to take (or not take) concerted activity.

Bathroom-line solidarity: After a long community-wide battle to stop a tool-manufacturing company from shutting down and moving the factory, the company built a new factory—but extracted a wage freeze from workers.

The four-year contract also kept incentive rates static. Workers had taken concessions, while the company's profits were soaring.

Stewards can bend the rules without getting anyone fired.

After two years of this, the workers and the union had had enough. Union leaders pushed workers to begin a campaign to convince the company to reopen the contract and end the wage freeze.

The campaign had several parts. Incentive workers followed the contract exactly and produced enough parts to meet the 100 percent rate. Most workers had previously produced a lot more, but now the company was receiving 30-40 percent less production.

At break and lunch times, workers would line up at the bathrooms and at the pay phones to call home. At times there would be lines of 100 workers. Of course, not every worker could make their call or use the facilities during the 15-minute break or 20-minute lunch.

The lines remained after the breaks were over. Supervisors would order people back to work, but this would take time, as many workers would patiently explain to the boss why they needed to call home (sick kids, spouse emergency) or why they needed to use the bathroom.

If directly ordered they would politely agree and return to work, or leave and then get back in line, ready with a new explanation if the boss should confront them again.

These actions continued for six months every single day, until the company agreed to reopen the contract.

WHAT DID THE UNION DO RIGHT?

Everything. The company never got a chance to discipline anyone for insubordination. No one ever told a boss to go to hell or refused a direct order. Participation was never 100 percent, but workers did not turn the fight on themselves. They remained focused on the company.

WHISTLING DOWN THE BOSS

Workers at a window factory were extremely mad at the owners. Managers refused to discuss grievances seriously and were harassing many workers. They decided that action was needed to make management deal fairly with them.

One day at lunch time, the entire factory marched into the offices, blowing whistles, chanting slogans, and carrying signs. The secretaries looked on in disbelief.

Management came out and tried to talk to the union rep, but he wouldn't talk. The boss shouted an order for people to go back to work, but the noise was so great no one could hear him.

The workers' 20-minute lunch period ended and no one returned to work. Soon the bosses began going up to each worker and ordering him or her back to work. Some left, others stayed. After about 10 minutes the remaining workers marched back to work and the union rep left the factory.

At the end of the day the company fired 10 workers for insubordination. These 10 had been the very last to leave the bosses' office.

The union filed a charge with the Labor Board that the firings were retaliation for protected activity, but the board ordered the union to arbitrate the case. The board's longstanding position is that unions should first arbitrate anything that could possibly come under the contract—like discharge for just cause.

> **If the union pulls an action during a break, keep an eye on the clock.**

Station Casino workers in Las Vegas bring a petition to the boss.

At the hearing the union rep and some of the workers were clearly hostile to the company and aggressively proud of what they'd done.

The arbitrator did not react well. He made it clear he did not like the whistle-blowing, the disrupting of the secretaries who were not on lunch break, the refusal to follow the bosses' orders, and the overstaying of the lunch break.

He admitted workers had a right to protest and to blow whistles and chant slogans. He reluctantly acknowledged that workers had the right to protest inside the factory while on break.

But he singled out the union rep for disrupting the secretaries and preventing them from working. Workers had overstayed their break and many of them refused a direct order to return to work.

His solution was to return seven of the 10 to work and uphold the dismissal of three union leaders who were the last to leave the bosses' office (and were the most macho on the stand). The union's appeal to the board was unsuccessful.

WHAT SHOULD THE UNION REP HAVE DONE DIFFERENTLY?

- Not marched into an area where other workers would be disrupted.
- Kept a close eye on the clock and made sure everyone was back to work before the break was over.

- When the boss gave a direct order, he should have tried to discuss it with him. If that didn't work, he should have smiled and switched tactics.

Understand that one action usually doesn't win the day. It takes persistence to win.

TURNING AN ISSUE INTO A CAMPAIGN

by Ellen David Friedman

Sandi walks up to you, the steward, just as the hallways start filling with noisy high schoolers heading for the bus. She is ready to blow her top, and over the din she tells you her supervisor is demanding that she continue driving special education students in her own car—long a part of her job as a teaching assistant—despite a recent warning from her insurance agent that she's not covered for it.

"He told me if I refuse to drive, I'm fired," she says. "I've been in this job seven years, never any problem. Can he do that?"

The goal is not just to help members solve problems, but to build collective self-confidence and power.

You've been a steward long enough to know the routine. You ask Sandi: "Why don't you write up the facts of what happened? Include what your supervisor said, what led up to the conversation, whether there were witnesses. Include what your insurance agent said, your job description, how long you've been driving.

"Then look through the contract. Check under the insurance section, reimbursement for out-of-pocket expenses, right to refuse work...anything that might be relevant. Then let's go talk to your supervisor together, and if we can't get it fixed, look into filing a grievance."

And then, because you are a great steward, one who wants to build union power from the bottom up, you ask Sandi one more question: "Anyone else in the same situation?" And that question could change everything. Now you are on your way to "turning an issue into a campaign."

Not all issues are worthy of a campaign, of course. If Sandi reports that other teaching assistants aren't affected, the savvy steward could still find strategic ways to use a grievance to build the union. That's a topic for another day, however.

BUILDING A CAMPAIGN

Grievances, while necessary tools, can make workplace problems seem like individual problems rather than collective ones that can be solved through collective action.

Ask Sandi to talk to her co-workers: How many other people are assigned to drive students? How often do they drive? What does their job description say about driving? Does everyone use their own car? What were employees told about car insurance? Have they talked to their own insurance agents?

With an informal database, Sandi can keep track of which co-workers she's talked to, what they said, and where the information gaps are. Most importantly, encourage Sandi to tell the other assistants they'll all need to get together and talk about how to solve this problem.

This approach has several purposes: It gets Sandi active and organizing, putting the issue on co-workers' radar screens. It educates members, and shows them that the union is paying attention to what goes on in their lives. It makes the "fact checking" phase of the campaign a dynamic and two-way process. And it produces the documentation needed to move into the action phase.

As the campaign organizer, your goal is not just to help members solve their workplace problems but to help them build collective self-confidence and power. A campaign is just a series of steps that help people focus on a common issue, identify a solution, and build pressure on the person with the power to solve the problem.

DEEP AND WIDE?

The next step is to assess whether this is a problem that is deeply felt (important enough to do something about) and widely felt (a majority of those who could be affected are affected).

Let's say Sandi comes back with a few other teaching assistants in tow, and they are fuming. It turns out that most are driving students on a regular basis, and none have been told that all liability is on their personal insurance.

Now your task is to help members clearly define the problem and articulate a winnable solution. Get the assistants together for a union meeting to weigh the pros and cons of different approaches. Sandi leads off, summarizing the facts she and her co-workers have gathered in face-to-face meetings, phone calls, and surveys. "We've now got information from 37 out of 42 assistants," says Sandi. "It's really a strong case."

The results of this careful effort showed that 80 percent of the workers were driving students in their own cars, with no insurance provided by the employer. "But we found one interesting exception," Sandi explained.

"One gal went to the supervisor—like two years ago—and said she'd only drive if the district covered her under its policy. So they did—but they said she couldn't tell anyone else." Everyone's ears perked up at that news. One member pointed out that if they were all talking to each other more, they would have figured this out a lot sooner.

THE RIGHT KIND OF PLAN

The meeting gets really lively at this point, as the members debate solutions and strategies. As steward, your job is to raise questions and criteria that will help the members reach consensus on a plan: What can we do that will actively involve the members—a petition, a mass meeting with the supervisor, a job action, what else?

What are the possible impacts and risks of each of these actions? Who are our allies? What's the outcome we're looking for? Who has the power to make this happen?

By the meeting's end there will be a plan with a series of accelerating tactics written out on a timeline, which will keep the members actively engaged and increase pressure on the boss to solve the problem. Before things break up, you make sure everyone knows their tasks, agrees to report back, and keeps in touch to adjust the plan as things unfold.

Of course, Sandi wants you to file a grievance, too. But now it will be a group grievance, presented en masse to the supervisor during her lunch break, accompanied by a delegation of supportive teacher union members, with a tape recorder running. When you turn an issue into a campaign, grievances become a tool for building union power.

WHEN BAD GRIPES HAPPEN TO GOOD STEWARDS

by Ellen David Friedman

Healthy unions should welcome workplace discontent. Stewards can turn discontent into campaigns that build workplace power.

Sometimes, though, too much *unproductive discontent* is floating around. Maybe there's a culture that supports bitching but no action; maybe there are tensions among co-workers that prevent cooperation.

Here's a look at two cases and what a steward can do:

The paralyzed griper. Sofia has been riled up over a pay grade problem for months, and you have heard every chapter of the saga. She feels she's been assigned work above her grade, but isn't being paid accordingly.

The supervisor won't support her application for an upgrade without documentation. But Sofia's dragged her feet because she'd have to prove that her work is different from co-workers in her pay grade, and she's too uncomfortable to actually ask them to describe their work in detail.

She can't file a grievance until she's applied for an upgrade and been denied. If she refuses the assigned work, she thinks she might be found insubordinate or stuck where she is forever.

Sofia's kind of paralyzed, and her co-workers are really tense about it, too. The problem here is that co-workers don't talk freely with each other about their work; a mood of underlying competition or distrust dominates. As steward, you may have to introduce some new standards into the workplace.

Consider a survey that asks detailed information about actual job duties compared to job title (reassuring members that it's anonymous).

Lots of complaints but no action? Maybe it's time for an (anonymous) survey.

Then compile the results and post them on the union bulletin board, with some pointed questions:

Are you constantly assigned new responsibilities with no change in pay?

Should you be upgraded to a higher job title?

Is this happening to everyone or just some of us?

Have you read what the contract says about job upgrades?

Are we better off "just getting by" or should we be "going somewhere"?

GET THEM TALKING

After you get a little buzz going, you could call an informational meeting about the process for job upgrades. Set a comfortable, non-judgmental tone.

Remind members that they are setting precedents for each other which are either bad (allowing standards to remain low and meaningless) or good (forcing the boss to follow the rules and move people up). Remind them that the goal isn't to compete against each other for the same slice of pie, but to cooperate and build strength together to demand a bigger pie.

Once folks have started to share their stories, it may come out that there are inequities—and these can be uncomfortable to face. Your task is to depersonalize the situation, pointing out that the job of the union isn't to evaluate workers but to make sure the contract is followed.

Help members talk to each other non-judgmentally. Build a sense of shared purpose by moving action along on behalf of affected groups, where possible, rather than individuals.

Doing all of this openly will not only break the tension between co-workers but signal to the boss that things are changing. When the pay grade problems get fixed, what a great confidence-builder for members!

NO GRIEVANCE HERE

Then there's the privileged griper. When Nate asks to talk with you, it's a welcome surprise; he's a respected and influential employee, but he's never been involved in the union. But your enthusiasm fades as Nate lays out an elaborate history of conflict with an upper-level boss who he believes has thwarted his career advancement.

It turns out that Nate has tried—on his own, never consulting the union—to cut deals with various bosses to move up, but has always been stymied. Now he wants to turn it all over to you, making it clear this is his "test" of the union: "After all these years of paying dues, if you can't do something for me, I'll make sure everyone knows how useless the union is."

A review of the facts makes it clear there is no contract violation, no disparate treatment, no breach of due process…in short, nothing grievable. You may be tempted to file a grievance, do your best, and let Nate lose. But he's likely to lash out against the union. If you reject his request, the result will be the same. So, let's consider some options.

No matter what else, make sure to keep Nate fully apprised of what you're doing. Let him see your activity on his behalf.

Let Nate know you'll have to share some facts of his case, as a condition of proceeding. This is normal because every case has precedent-setting power and may affect the rights of others.

Find some other members who share the respected status that Nate enjoys and who may have similar job frustrations. Ask their opinions. Walk them through the grievance criteria to help them see why you're reluctant to proceed. If they, too, see the absence of merit, then you've found some allies in case Nate blows up.

Next step is to ask Nate to write a summary of his case, including the contract clause he's claiming and the proposed remedy, and give it to the Grievance Committee.

(No Grievance Committee? Now's the time to constitute one and train its members as both advocates and dispassionate gatekeepers of the process.)

Invite Nate to present his case to them, possibly inviting other union leaders to attend, so as to add gravitas to the ultimate decision. At this session, be prepared to let Nate down respectfully and instead generate brainstorming about non-grievance solutions. If you've learned there are others facing the same problem, get them involved in strategizing and use the union's resources to carry out a plan.

Even if Nate drops it at this stage, you will have blunted any criticism by showing him respect, engaging other members, calling on the institutional strengths of the union, and generating creative alternatives to a grievance.

If he still tries to rile up anti-union feeling, it will ring pretty hollow.

Chapter Two

BARGAINING

It's Time for Management Concessions, The Labor Institute, 1983.

MID-CONTRACT CONCESSIONS: WHAT TO DO?

by Richard de Vries

Every day it's front page news. Another company closes, big unions take concessions, municipal workers go on furlough. The boss puts your members through a one-hour PowerPoint on competition in China and India. The day arrives when he asks for concessions. How do bargainers respond?

THE GROUND RULES

The first question to ask is: what happens if the parties cannot agree? In normal bargaining an impasse allows management to impose an agreement unilaterally. Impasses can be broken by strikes, corporate campaigns, boycotts, or on-the-job actions that cause the company to change its mind and keep talking.

If givebacks have to happen, get something in return.

In midterm bargaining, though, with a contract in place, a no-strike, no-lockout clause is usually in effect. Slowdowns and other actions are difficult. Does the company think that it can claim impasse and impose its terms? If so, don't re-open.

The second rule for concession bargaining is total transparency. Members need to know what sacrifices management is making. The union needs complete access to the books for verification of management's claims. If the company is not willing to allow total transparency, there should be no concessions.

ARE CONCESSIONS NEEDED?

Next, the union must test the company's need for concessions. The Supreme Court has ruled that if the employer claims the inability to pay, the argument "is important enough to require some proof of its accuracy." The union has the legal right to check the books.

Write a letter asking for a detailed accounting of income, expenses, profits, and losses for six previous years. Request copies of the IRS

W-3 and the IRS 1096, and give assurances of security concerning proprietary and confidential information.

Say that the union isn't rejecting the opening proposal, but needs to verify the underlying information that demonstrates the company's inability to meet its obligations. If the union does recommend that members reject, that call should be based on examined facts.

A number of employers faced with a demand to see the books change their tune from "need concessions" to "want concessions."

The key to good-faith bargaining is a reliable source reviewing the books. During crisis bargaining with YRC, the largest union freight carrier, the Teamsters secured an outside consulting firm to thoroughly review YRC's operations.

The depth review was beyond what the Labor Board may have supported, because it looked at every management and non-union salary, benefit, stock holding, and bonus, as well as terminal management, routing of freight, and the customer base. The review became a neutral source of data for both sides.

HOW DEEP A CONCESSION?

The question then becomes, how deep is the trouble and what kind of fix are we bargaining about? Don't trust the employer's math; do your own costing.

In recent bargaining at a Teamster trucking company, the employer said it could not afford the pending health and welfare and pension increase of $40 a week. To break even, the employer was asking for a dollar an hour off the wages.

The union pulled time cards for the last six months and found drivers were averaging 14 to 20 hours a week in overtime. With overtime, the original proposal would have taken up to $70 a week off wages. Probably a concession of 65 to 70 cents would have put the company at break-even.

The union also pointed out that any reduction in wages reduces taxes the employer pays. On a 65-cent wage cut, the company would probably save 12 to 16 cents. In reality, the company needed only a 50-cent cut.

Make any givebacks temporary: in this case, the union made the cut for one year, with the contract popping back to pre-concession wage scales.

> ## DO CONCESSIONS WORK?
>
> When employers catch a break on labor costs, the bottom line looks better. But do concessions meet any of labor's goals? Do they even fix management's needs? Do they help non-union workers?
>
> They don't affect an economic crisis brought on by wild speculation in the banking and investment sector, or poor management, or global competition. They don't prevent job loss, or bring back outsourced jobs, or fix broken unions that have not organized for years.
>
> When the union firm takes a dollar-an-hour cut, the non-union company cuts its wages $1.10 and starts chasing the customer to switch vendors.
>
> Concessions need to be looked at case by case, but they do not fix a company's root problems. In the end concessions should be resisted because they hurt the union community at large as well as the non-union worker.

THE QUID PRO QUO

No contract should be reopened without getting something for it—this is the union's card to play when the company says concessions are urgent. Open the contract beyond the money issues the employer wants—go for a total reopener.

As a first condition of bargaining, the union can ask to end the "zipper clause" that precludes either party from raising subjects of bargaining during the life of the agreement.

Make job preservation specific—not just a hope. This is your opportunity to get language that says "there shall be no subcontracting of bargaining unit work while unit employees are on layoff" or "there shall be no subcontracting of work which can be performed by the bargaining unit."

Fix that grievance definition. Often our contracts narrow the definition of a grievance to what is found inside the four corners of the contract, leaving out the flexibility to grieve and bargain over rapidly changing economic conditions. The union needs to secure the broadest rights to grieve in any situation.

Change your grievance definition to "any dispute over application and interpretation of this agreement and any other dispute over wages, hours, and other terms and conditions of employment."

GET A WARNING

The WARN Act, which requires 60-day notice of shutdowns, does not provide the cover we assumed it would. It works for employers of 100 or more (excluding part-timers) but not for smaller ones. If your facility is not covered, **shutdown-notice language is a must**.

If you can, insist that any shutdown be mutually agreed upon. Historically forbidden territory can now be entered. Over and over the NLRB has said the transfer, closing, or relocation of a facility is the God-given right of the employer and a permissive subject of bargaining. Now it's on the table. In exchange for concessions, the union should demand that nothing gets shuttered except by mutual agreement.

BIND THE SUCCESSOR

When a company is in crisis the **"successors and assigns" language should be strengthened**. Here's some sample language:

> *The terms and provisions of this agreement shall bind all sub-lessees, assignees, purchasers or other successors to the business to such terms and provisions, to which the employees are and shall continue to be entitled. The employer shall require any purchaser, transferee, lessee, assignee, receiver, or trustee of the operations covered by this agreement to accept the terms of the agreement by written notice, a copy of which shall be provided to the local union at least 30 days prior to the effective date of any sale, transfer, lease assignment, receivership, or bankruptcy proceedings.*

Legally, it is hard to bind the next owner without its consent. The party that is bound is the current employer. Hold his feet to the fire before any sale by forcing a written pre-notice. This allows the union a chance to mobilize the community and politicians, as well as to seek an injunction to block the transfer if the new owner does not accept the contract.

Layoff and recall language needs to be improved to secure longer return rights. An easy fix for many contracts is to change language to protect members for "12 months, or a period equal to the employee's seniority, whichever is *greater*."

BARGAINING TACTICS FOR PENSIONS

by David Cohen

The retirement system in our country is under attack. Every day we hear of large corporations terminating their defined-benefit pension plans and replacing them with a 401(k) or other defined-contribution plan that will give employees a lower standard of living when they retire.

In every recent United Electrical Workers (UE) negotiation, whether in the private or public sector, the workers have faced demands to pay more for health insurance and to take cuts in their pension plans. Our response has been to step up our educational programs for members on how to bargain, fight for, and defend pensions and health insurance.

Employers will try to prey on members' focus on the here and now to crimp their future.

Stewards are crucial in preparing for negotiations on pensions. Stewards must play a key role in making sure the members understand how their pensions work, why making the employer put money into the pension plan is important, and how much money they will need to retire.

For many members, pensions are not an immediate issue. Their own retirement may be 20 or 30 years in the future. Today they are faced with paying rent, car payments, or mortgages, buying food and clothes for children, or making health insurance payments.

Many employers understand this and try to play the long term off against the short term. The problem is that each year without a pension improvement is lost forever.

TIPS FOR BARGAINING

When it comes to bargaining, prepare in advance—far in advance. Discussion with the members about the importance of improving their pensions should not wait until negotiations are underway.

Retirement experts like to talk about the three-legged stool of retirement, each leg representing one third of your retirement income. One leg is Social Security, another is your employer-funded pension, and the last is your own savings. They also estimate that workers will need about 70 percent of their pre-retirement earnings to live on while retired.

As we hope our incomes grow through negotiations, so must our pensions grow, so that they will provide their share of the three-legged stool.

If you have a defined-benefit pension plan, ask the employer for a copy of the annual Form 5500 they must file with the IRS. This will show you how well your pension is funded, or how much it is underfunded. These forms can also be downloaded from www.FreeErisa.com.

Besides negotiating an increase in your pension plan formula, you can also negotiate that the pension plan will provide joint and survivor options with no reduction in your monthly pension benefits. When you elect to leave part of your pension to your spouse after you die, normally your monthly pension is reduced to pay for this benefit.

If you have a defined-contribution plan, try to negotiate increases in the employer's contributions. Defined-contribution plans are not as secure as defined-benefit plans, because they depend on the ups and downs of the stock market, and employers are not responsible for making up lost funds. The employer should pay all administrative costs of a defined-contribution plan.

The UE estimates that workers will need 12-15 percent of their income going into a defined-contribution plan, over a long period of time, in order to provide enough money for them to retire on.

Do not agree to company stock as the employer's contribution to your pension plan. Remember Enron.

DEFINED-CONTRIBUTION PLANS

If the employer demands to terminate a defined-benefit plan and start a defined-contribution plan, resist at all costs. If you cannot, consider the following:

By examining years of 5500 reports, you can find out how much your employer has actually put into the pension plan. From there you can get a rough estimate of how much per hour the plan has cost. Don't settle for any less from a 401(k) or other contribution-type plan.

In our experience, employers offer plans that will cost them 50 percent less than they were spending on a defined-benefit plan.

Because almost all studies have shown that current defined-contribution plans provide inadequate pension benefits, people are beginning to recognize that more is needed. The Pension Protection Act of 2006 (which adversely affected most defined-benefit plans) included new pension plans called Hybrid Plans. They are part defined-benefit and part defined-contribution. Do some research—they would probably be better then the 401(k) plan your boss is offering.

The final task of the steward is to educate the members about the need for an adequate national retirement system in this country.

BARGAINING FOR HEALTH INSURANCE

by Peter Knowlton

One of a negotiating committee's biggest challenges is holding on to affordable health insurance. The latest attempt to chisel our coverage is "lower-cost" high-deductible plans and Health Savings Accounts—which make us pay huge up-front deductibles.

The industry calls these "consumer-driven" plans, but that Cadillac we've been accused of driving is really just a rusted-out Chevy.

Unions are faced with resisting more restrictive networks, gatekeeper systems, higher and higher co-pays, tiered systems for prescription drugs, deletion of coverage for certain procedures such as chiropractic care, and gigantic up-front deductibles—all offered with the carrot of lower premium costs.

The local needs up-to-date information on members' health care needs to avoid getting them into serious financial trouble.

But any lower costs are short-lived. It is the exact same argument the industry used to get unions to switch from fee-for-service to HMOs.

In the United Electrical Workers (UE), workshops on how to grapple with health insurance are popular at conventions and meetings. We teach some basic principles:

- No paperwork
- Choice of provider
- Affordable and fair payroll deductions for insurance
- Low or no out-of-pocket costs
- No high co-pays or deductibles
- Changes must be negotiated and any increased costs to workers must be reimbursed by the employer.
- Any "self-administration" or time spent handling insurance problems should be done during work time.

These days employers want to foist off on workers the administration of their insurance. Where we used to go to the front office to get help from Human Resources, now we are given a phone number ("call 1-800-UR-SCREWD"). Locals should not let members or union officials be forced to take care of insurance issues on their own time.

Contract language must protect against insurance changes during the life of the agreement. No year goes by when the company does not claim the carrier is "mandating" changes to the plan (increased co-pays, ending coverage for certain procedures). This is BS, because a company can have any insurance it wants, as long as it pays for it.

Language such as "the new carrier or plan must provide comparable coverage and network" leaves the employer an opening as big as a house. Language that says the new plan must provide "identical" or "equal" coverage gives greater protection.

Best yet is to have the insurance plan and coverage levels written directly into the contract, with no language concerning how it could be changed. Then the plan holds for the life of the agreement.

SURVEY YOUR MEMBERS

A system with co-pays for this and deductibles for that means we must know the membership and everyone's particular situation. The variation among plans means that if the local does not have up-to-date information on members' needs, it could potentially put some in serious financial trouble.

In many UE locals the membership is thoroughly surveyed: Who are their doctors? What types of prescription drugs are members and families using?

Our experience is that most folks are OK with giving out this information, to help keep insurance affordable, as long as the company isn't in on it.

The idea is not to pry into members' health conditions but to be able to gauge the effect of changes in coverage. Especially in shops with older workers, even seemingly small increases to prescription or other co-pays could mean hundreds and maybe thousands of dollars in additional expense.

Surveys have also enabled us to better figure out the annual cost difference to members from one plan to another, what members are paying now in premiums, co-pays, and deductibles versus what the proposed plan would mean.

Getting the employer to refund up-front deductibles can sometimes make a high-deductible plan cost less to a member over the course of a year than the premium deductions and increasing co-pays of an HMO. But we shouldn't make any switch without solid information on the effect on each member.

MAKING PAYMENT MORE JUST

Another issue is how we pay for health insurance. Traditionally we have deducted from our paychecks a certain percentage of the premium or, in some cases, the employer pays for the single plan and we are responsible for the difference that a family plan costs. People with families bear a disproportionate share of the cost.

Many UE locals have been setting caps on how much comes out of workers' paychecks, or flattening out the paycheck-deduction difference between single, two-person, and family plans. Basing our paycheck deductions on premium rates leaves us hostage to industry profits and market forces over which we exercise little control. Paying a percentage of income for health care is less risky and more equitable.

The University of Vermont, for example, where UE represents custodial and maintenance workers, bases the premium on a wage rate range. Employees who make the least pay the lowest percentage of the insurance premium and those who make more pay higher percentages.

A final note on a tactic some UE locals have been using to "make trouble." We present the employer with a letter to sign: "We, _Name of employer,_ support the only viable solution to the continuing crisis in health care—a single-payer public health insurance program for all _name of state_ residents and the passage of legislation supporting the same."

Not surprisingly, 99 percent of the time the employer refuses to sign. That's "socialism," they say—despite its reduction in cost to the employer by nearly two-thirds. As we report to the membership the company's crocodile tears over its insurance costs, we let members know the company has no interest in supporting a real solution to the nation's health care woes and we, therefore, have little sympathy for its premium plight.

We need to use our negotiations to force employers to face this question. And we need to educate members on the unsustainability of our present private health insurance system and the need to secure a universal, single-payer system of health care for everyone.

[For a sample survey and sample single-payer letter for employers (as well as a PowerPoint presentation on health care costs and union strategies), go to www.uenortheast.org and click "UE documents."]

BARGAIN TO ORGANIZE, ORGANIZE TO BARGAIN

by Matt Luskin

The labor movement has long debated its priority: organize new members or represent the ones we have? Our local has found that we grow *because of* the strength of current members. We have had to do both—be strong in our organized shops and grow through new organizing—or we could do neither.

Six thousand workers at Help At Home, a for-profit home health care company based in Chicago, were organized in SEIU Healthcare. They travelled to the homes of low-income seniors to provide cooking, housekeeping, and other non-medical care, largely paid for by the state.

Although workers had won improvements through the union, they had a rocky relationship with the company. Near-minimum wages for a time became bounced paychecks. Help At Home went through bankruptcy, questions often went unanswered, and grievances or actions were needed for the most routine of items, such as receiving annual raises.

In 2008, Help At Home was about to receive the largest funding increase ever to its state contracts. Union leaders knew this was a chance to get a substantial raise—$1 an hour—and to access new state funding for employees' health insurance. But we began to consider how much more power we would have if we organized the company nationally.

Help At Home activists across Illinois, union leaders, and staff began discussing what could happen if we added national organizing rights to our Illinois bargaining demands. When workers had made an attempt to organize in several states the previous year, the company quickly brought in anti-union consultants and held captive audience meetings. The campaigns fizzled, for the moment.

Members can mobilize at contract time on behalf of other workers who want a union.

The options were a quick contract settlement with the new state funding, a fairly sure thing that would benefit Illinois workers but leave us with the same disappointing relationship with Help At Home. Or a riskier strategy: to demand expanded organizing rights in other states alongside our economic demands in Illinois, in the hope of dramatically increasing our power with the boss.

The bargaining committee wanted to see Help At Home workers organized nationally. Many of them had led organizing drives at their own shops. They knew the promise of quick raises for Illinois employees would be tempting to many workers and that they would have to build connections with those just starting to organize in Indiana.

CONNECTING THE DEMANDS

Members wanted to demonstrate to the company that organizing rights in Indiana would be central to an Illinois settlement. From the first day, every piece of literature we distributed included a demand to end union-busting in Indiana alongside our demands for Illinois raises and health insurance. Bargaining updates to union members included reports on the company's anti-union activities in other states.

Help At Home workers had regularly used direct actions in previous contract campaigns. This time, workers coordinated short takeovers of eight Illinois Help At Home branches on the same day, with the demand to end union-busting. They delivered thousands of postcards from members pledging support to their co-workers in Indiana.

On paycheck pick-up days, union activists and staff would provide cell phones for workers to fill the voicemail boxes of company executives with hundreds of messages of solidarity with Indiana. Indiana managers received messages from Illinois workers demanding they end their anti-union activities.

For the Indiana workers, reports of this activity across the border encouraged them during difficult organizing drives.

Direct connections were also built. Many Illinois members volunteered time house-visiting across the border. A few went on leave to work full-time on the campaign. Others made calls from their union halls or homes to talk to Indiana workers who had not made up their minds.

COMPANY PUSHES BACK

The company claimed that Illinois and Indiana were "separate issues." Leaflets to Illinois members claimed management was ready to hand out $1 raises immediately, and that the union was keeping them from doing it.

A company flyer with the name and photo of a leading bargaining committee member was released, implying she thought workers should take the raise. But workers remained remarkably invested in the Indiana organizing.

Members of the Indiana organizing committees were invited to sit on the Illinois bargaining committee. While they were officially non-voting, advisory participants, their presence sent a message to Help At Home.

They also gave Illinois workers firsthand accounts of their organizing (and management's activity). They inspired the Illinois members to keep building support for "no settlement without Indiana."

Most important, sitting on the bargaining committee allowed the Indiana workers to see the union in action. They saw rank-and-file leaders fighting and winning. They saw management being confronted by militant, organized workers and having to take it.

NOT JUST US

Management's strategy had been based on the belief that Illinois workers would care only about how much of a raise they received and how quick. Executives believed organizing rights were just a union officers' issue. The company never believed that significant numbers of workers would care what happened to non-union employees they would never meet.

They were taken by surprise. One executive told union leaders, "I can't walk into our offices anywhere in Illinois without getting yelled at about it!"

The Illinois workers emerged with a contract that provided their largest raises ever, health insurance for the first time, and other improvements. And Help At Home signed an agreement that expanded the organizing rights of thousands of workers in the other states where the company operates. Since then more than 600 Help At Home workers have won organizing drives, and more campaigns are underway.

The lessons from this campaign were soon applied again. The Indiana workers campaigning for their first contract in 2010 returned the favor to Illinois workers. Indiana bargaining sessions included Illinois workers who advised, supported, and coordinated activity across the company.

At the same time, thousands of Illinois workers, about to head into their own contract bargaining, signed petitions demanding a fair settlement in both states or a battle in Illinois.

MORE ON ORGANIZING

There's much more about organizing existing members and workers new to the union in Chapter 5. A series of three articles explains how to form a stewards council and put it to use winning campaigns and uniting many types of workers to defend the most vulnerable.

Other authors profile unions that had sudden influxes of new members and found ways to involve them in leadership.

And finally, many unions are now organizing in right-to-work states or under similar conditions, where membership levels are always stressed. In an era where more unions face the loss of dues check-off, they offer advice on how to use dues collection not just to keep the organization functioning but to advance members' involvement in the union's struggles.

MAKE TECHNOLOGY WORK FOR US, NOT AGAINST US

by Charley Richardson

The stress and pressure to work faster in a modern call center, said a CWA local president recently, goes so far that workers are in some cases forbidden to say please or thank you because it takes too long.

This intensity is created by technologies that continuously monitor call center workers, limit their interaction with both co-workers and clients, and de-skill the workforce through mind-numbing standardization of work.

A member of the Massachusetts Nurses Association said electronic medical records, remote-control health care, and employee monitoring systems have cascaded into workplaces, in part due to more than $19 billion from the federal stimulus. The monitoring includes active badges that track nurses wherever they go in the hospital.

And UPS drivers are subjected to telematics, a system that combines data from the driver's handheld computer, GPS, and more than 200 sensors mounted on the truck, used to track workers throughout their day and increase their workload. From how fast they are going and how often they drive in reverse to whether they have their seat belt fastened and their door locked, management has access to a detailed electronic map of a driver's day.

BECAUSE THEY CAN

Technologies make it easier and easier for management to intrude into, and therefore control, our lives at work. They are monitoring us because they can, and because we haven't stood in their way.

Why is management so interested in keeping such a close eye on workers? The big myth is that monitoring is primarily designed to catch "cheaters"—people who take too long in the bathroom, who wander where they "shouldn't" (including on the internet), or who aren't doing their work, or enough of it. As a result, much of the contract language that exists is about limiting the use of monitoring information for discipline.

Monitoring is indeed used to catch people, which increases the amount of discipline stewards have to deal with and the difficulty of protecting those who get caught—video and computer printouts are hard to counter in front of an arbitrator. Members need to understand what monitoring is capable of, clearly.

> If unions don't bargain aggressively, technology is used to erode power and intensify work.

But this view leads some to think that if you're doing your job, you don't have to be concerned. That misses the point. Management doesn't spend the kind of money it spends on monitoring just to catch a few slackers.

Management monitors to gather data so it can analyze the work process and intensify it. They use data to cut corners, speed workers up, increase stress, and eliminate jobs.

HOW TO COUNTER IT

Unfortunately, unions are mostly failing to take on the technologies management is introducing.

New technologies can affect the number of jobs, the skills needed, training issues, pace of work, intensity of work, control over the work process, and even the ability to do our work well. Nurses, for example, complain that electronic medical records are interfering with direct patient contact ("we're looking at the screen instead of the patient") and often don't easily provide the information that they need to give the best care quickly.

Few contracts have language on technology that gives the union clear rights. In fact, management usually uses the management rights clause when introducing new technologies, which they think gives them a free hand.

So what do we need to know?

We do have rights. At least in workplaces covered by the National

Labor Relations Act or similar state laws, management rights clauses do not take away our right to bargain during the life of the contract. If the technology has an impact on mandatory subjects of bargaining, including job descriptions, training, workload, and health and safety, it's up for debate.

But we need to take the initiative because our rights disappear if we don't demand to bargain as soon as we know about the new technologies and their potential impacts.

It's about power. Most new technologies in the workplace tip power toward management. If we accept that change without challenge, technologies will continue to be designed and implemented in ways that hurt workers.

We need to change how we think about technology. The feeling that there is nothing you can do about technology is very strong. We've been told that technology is "progress," that it preserves competitiveness and therefore jobs, and that it is simply inevitable. These myths make it difficult to rally folks for a fight.

In reality, technology could do the opposite of what it does to workers now. It could be implemented in ways that improve health and safety, make our jobs easier, and upgrade skills, all while improving productivity.

But, since this is capitalism, this will not happen if our voices are excluded from the discussion. Instead, technology will be used against us.

We need to take action. If you're not at the table, you'll be on the menu. The good news is that we have plenty of opportunities for action.

Stewards and other shop floor leaders can:

1. Catch Up: Examine the impacts new technologies have had or may have on the workforce and the union. If technology is not easy for you to get your head around, find someone else in the local who understands it or wants to learn. This can be a way to turn more people into activists.

2. Educate: Use the experience within your local or others to educate members about the impacts and begin discussing a union campaign to bargain over technology. Contact the university-based labor program in your area, if there is one, to get help. Remember, you don't have to understand all the details about how the technology works, just how it could be used in your workplace. Calling a special union meeting to have a discussion with members can be a great way to build understanding, create involvement, and put the company on notice.

3. Organize: Set up a technology committee to monitor tech changes, research their impacts, and represent the union in discussions. This committee should talk with members from different departments and classifications to hear about changes that might be coming down the pike.

Tell members to keep an eye open for new wires being installed, vendors coming in, machines or workstations being moved. The committee can gather information on the new technologies identified, help develop information requests and bargaining demands to submit to management, and put together an organizing and bargaining plan.

4. Bargain: Always put in a formal demand to bargain as soon as the union discovers a potential new technology, along with an information request. Then go to work building a campaign in support.

You won't always get everything you want, but you can soften the blow, bring new skilled work into the bargaining unit, and lay the basis for more struggle in the future.

Fighting management's domination of technology can create a real discussion about control over our jobs and a challenge to the dogma of management rights that is so destructive to the labor movement.

JUST SAY 'NO' TO DRUG TESTS— THEN BARGAIN

by David Cohen

Under the guise of concern for employees' safety and health, employers demand the right to conduct drug and alcohol testing. Most use it as just another hammer to hold over workers' heads.

Employers often try to divide the membership on this issue, since the overwhelming majority don't drink or use drugs on the job. We can turn this around by pointing out, "Why subject the majority to testing if only a few people may have problems?" We then can unite the members around fighting for a no-testing policy. If it looks like we can't win that, then we make the fight for the best, least harassing policy.

A good policy limits management's intrusiveness and recognizes addiction as as an illness.

When the company informs you that it intends to start a testing program for all employees, what are the union's rights?

Can the company implement a change of this nature mid-contract?

No. The employer does not have the right to unilaterally make such a large change in working conditions. But as with all mid-contract bargaining, it is up to the union to demand bargaining.

Does the company then have to bargain over drug testing?

Yes, if the union makes the demand. The National Labor Relations Board ruled in 1987 that "drug testing for current employees and job applicants is a mandatory subject of bargaining," adding that "a union's waiver of its bargaining rights must be clear and unmistakable."

The NLRB has ruled that just filing a grievance is not the same as demanding bargaining. The union must put it in writing: "Local 946 demands that the employer enter into negotiations over its proposed drug and alcohol testing program, and the employer must immediately stop any drug and alcohol testing of union employees that it may have started."

Can the union "just say no"?

If we take the position that we'll simply grieve any unjust discipline under the "just cause" clause, we'll end up with a policy that is bad for members and will have a weaker position at arbitration over whether a firing was justified.

One tool is our right to demand information from the employer concerning why it wants to implement a testing program. The University of Iowa Labor Center has compiled a list of 125 questions and demands for information that unions can use. Examples:

- Exact information as to the employer's knowledge of any alleged drug or alcohol use in the workplace
- The economic impact of testing on the employer
- Training and knowledge supervisors have or will get to make them experts in spotting drug or alcohol abuse
- How management will ensure all information is kept confidential, and how the hospital or testing agency will guarantee the same
- How the employer can prove the tests are accurate. We want to see every scientific study in its entirety on the accuracy of each test
- If the employer claims drug and alcohol usage affects attendance, productivity, the employer's image, or employee accidents, then it must reveal all information to back this up, including every study used to back up this claim. This could include all data about every accident that happened over the course of years.

What kind of policy should be fought for?

No random testing.

Testing for **"just cause" or "reasonable cause" only**. These should be defined as slurred speech, inability to walk straight, erratic behavior, or other visual signs that would cause a reasonable person to believe the worker was under the influence. No automatic testing because of absence from work, an accident, being rude to a boss, or low production.

If an employee admits to having a problem, then no testing should be necessary and the only discussion should be on whether a rehab program is necessary.

Language should say that *on-the-job* **impairment** is unacceptable. We will accept tests that show on-the-job usage or impairment, not off-the-job usage. It is not the employer's place to be the "moral monitor" of off-the-job conduct.

In one case where the employer was insisting on this, the United Electrical Workers demanded the right to test the employer and supervisors for immoral acts they might take part in outside of work. The union proposed that all bosses take lie detector tests to see if they were racists. The employer soon agreed that testing would take place only if employees showed evidence of on-the-job impairment.

The employer must **provide transportation** to the testing facility and the worker must be paid for time missed from work.

Use **breathalyzer, saliva, or blood tests**. There is a difference in what the different tests show. Urine tests should be avoided, as these tests will show use of alcohol or drugs that occurs off the job and for weeks in the past. If urine testing is agreed to, then the levels of alcohol or other drugs present in the body must be set to show only current usage and impairment.

Breathalyzer tests for alcohol will show recent or on-the-job use. Blood testing also shows recent use, as does saliva testing for marijuana use.

Protect a worker's **right to privacy** while being tested. Always point out that the employee is innocent until proven guilty.

Negotiate the employee's right to have a **second test** done by a different agency using the same samples, at the employer's expense.

The agency doing the testing must be able to guarantee a safe **"chain of custody"** for the evidence. This means proof of who was handling the evidence at all times and proof that samples couldn't get mixed up with other samples. After a sample is given, the employee should sign the seal that closes the sample vial.

Get language that says rehabilitation is primary, not punishment. Employers must recognize alcoholism and drug addiction as illnesses. Employees should be allowed to use employee assistance programs that take place after work.

Only in extreme cases should an employee be made to leave work to attend a rehabilitation clinic. While at the clinic the employee should receive sickness and accident pay. The drug and alcohol policy must recognize that these illnesses are hard to cure and therefore termination can come only after a series of failed tests.

Does the Americans with Disabilities Act cover alcoholism or addiction?

Alcoholism is considered a disability only if the employee is actively undergoing treatment for it. In this case an employee should not be fired for being an alcoholic. This does not mean that the employee can come to work drunk, which could be a danger to other workers. The ADA excludes addiction to illegal drugs from consideration as a disability.

[Employees involved in transportation or repair of transportation vehicles may be covered under Department of Transportation rules which do include random drug testing.]

AN ADDITIONAL RESOURCE

The University of Iowa Labor Center's excellent "Alcohol and Drug Testing" manual gives detailed advice on dealing with such programs from start to finish. Iowa law is used, but most of the information applies to any union. Go to tiny.cc/drugtestmanual.

Chapter Three

RUNNING FOR OFFICE, RUNNING THE LOCAL

A reform caucus in the University of California graduate employees union won office after defeating a bid by incumbents to halt the ballot count.

BUILDING A TEAM TO WIN LOCAL UNION OFFICE

by William Johnson and Dan Lutz

Are you thinking about running for local union office?

If you're like most candidates, you start by asking, "Who can I get to run with me?"

It seems like a good question. But it's the wrong way to start your campaign.

What if one of the people on your slate turns out to be a dud? What if you meet new people who are better for the job or help you reach new voters?

That's why filling out your slate early usually isn't the best idea.

Besides, if you're in a big local, you're going to need a broad group of supporters helping you turn out the vote. You can't do that alone—even with your entire slate campaigning hard.

Candidates need a broad base of supporters, with varying levels of activity, high to low.

A better place to start is by building a broader *team* of members who will help you campaign, and pick your slate later in the game.

BIG AND SMALL COMMITMENTS

If you're running for office, you know what a big commitment the union can be: all the meetings, the early mornings, the late-night phone calls.

Most members aren't willing to be as committed as you are. They won't give up their weekends for the union. They won't wake up early to go hand out flyers.

That's OK. Even though most members won't commit as much as you do, some members are willing to do something.

Your job is to bring together the people who are willing to do a lot, and work with them to organize and mobilize the members who are willing to do a little.

YOUR CORE TEAM

Your core team is made up of the people who will distribute campaign leaflets, shirts, and stickers. They'll collect email addresses and phone numbers, sell raffle tickets, and phonebank members. They'll show up to important campaign events and come to some campaign meetings.

Ideally, your core team is bigger than your slate. Without this inner circle, you'll end up doing most of the campaign work yourself, and your campaign will suffer.

ACTIVE SUPPORTERS

There are usually many more members who won't come to many meetings, but who will help out where they work.

From the get-go, you want to recruit active supporters in key buildings and locations where you need votes. They can talk to other members about the campaign and introduce you to members when you're campaigning at their building. You can ask them to identify issues where they work and tell you who supports you in their shop. They should pass out flyers and wear campaign buttons and shirts. You should use their pictures and quotes endorsing you in campaign flyers.

Petitions are tools for getting people to talk member to member. They are not a substitute.

When the ballots are out, your active supporters can help you get out the vote across your local.

MAKING IT HAPPEN

It's hard to get members involved in our unions. So how do you get them involved in your campaign?

Make member-to-member contact the heart of your campaign. The most powerful organizing tool is talking to members one on one. Petitions, websites, and flyers are tools for getting people to talk member to member. They're no substitute.

Here are some more tips:

Map your local. Identify key shops and potential leaders. Then make a plan for getting those potential leaders more involved.

Start small. Don't overwhelm someone, especially when you are first trying to get him or her involved.

Make specific requests with a definite beginning and end. They're less intimidating. "Can you meet me from 7:30 to 9 to pass out leaflets

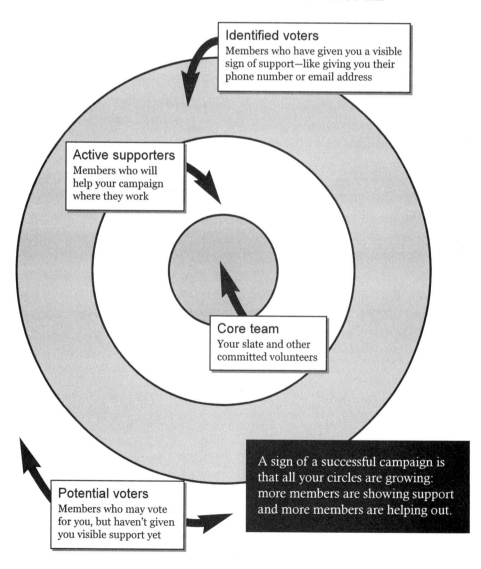

THE BULLSEYE CAMPAIGN MODEL

Identified voters
Members who have given you a visible sign of support—like giving you their phone number or email address

Active supporters
Members who will help your campaign where they work

Core team
Your slate and other committed volunteers

Potential voters
Members who may vote for you, but haven't given you visible support yet

A sign of a successful campaign is that all your circles are growing: more members are showing support and more members are helping out.

next Wednesday?" is better than "We need people who will help us reach other members."

Ask people to do things they do well—especially at first. As their confidence grows, so will their participation.

Tell each person how their job fits in with the rest. "Our goal is to reach members in every building with this leaflet in the next week. We have members covering A, B, and C locations. Can you cover D by Friday?"

Hold regular meetings for your core group. But don't confuse meetings with activity.

Ask supporters who can't come to meetings to help. More people will help you where they work than will come to your meetings.

Respect abilities and boundaries. Try to get people to take on more responsibility and get more involved, but remember not everyone will participate the same amount or in the same way.

Don't give up on people. If some members are potential assets to your campaign, keep talking to them and asking them to get involved. One "no" doesn't mean "never."

WHAT ABOUT MY SLATE?

There's a lot to think about when picking out your slate. Who is respected? Can you build alliances with other groups in the local? Can you build a team that represents the diversity of the local? And a lot more (it's a whole chapter in the authors' book, *Running for Local Union Office*).

Answering these questions will be a lot easier *after* you've started building your team and organizing for change in your local.

TO LEARN MORE

This article is adapted from *Running for Local Union Office*, a publication of Teamsters for a Democratic Union. This comprehensive guide covers building your team, campaign do's and don'ts, phone and email lists, flyers, mailers, websites, Facebook, fundraising, negative attacks, observing the vote count, and much more. Although the book is written for Teamsters, almost all of it will apply in any union election. Order at www.TDU.org/rfo.

ELECTION FLYERS THAT WIN VOTES

by William Johnson and Dan Lutz

When you're running for local union office, good campaign literature can help you tell members what you stand for and why you should you get their votes. But bad lit can make you look weak, defensive, whiny, unqualified, or all of the above.

How do you make the most of your election lit?

DO

Get help and advice from someone experienced. Ask winning candidates in other locals. Find folks with experience both in union politics and in design.

Keep it neat and clean. Effective literature does not have to look expensive. It should, however, look professional. You want the members to see that you're smart and competent; you don't want to give your opponents ammunition by passing out sloppy literature.

Use good photos, to show competence and professionalism.

Use photos and quotes from members who endorse you. Public support from a variety of members will impress voters.

Double-check all your facts. Your credibility is a big asset. Make sure each piece of literature is factual.

Translate your literature if your local has significant numbers of non-English speakers.

Focus on issues that interest all members, like pay, working conditions, benefits, and representation, rather than internal union questions.

DON'T

Don't make your lit all by yourself. Get someone else to help—and definitely get a second opinion on all the literature you put out, from people inside and outside your inner circle.

Don't be too negative. Some negative campaigning is appropriate, but too much can turn voters off. A good rule of thumb is to keep the criticisms to just 25 percent of your lit. Name-calling ("moron," "SOB") is never effective.

Don't criticize without offering solutions. Tell members how you will make things better, not just what your opponents have done to mess things up.

Don't be defensive. No doubt about it—your opponents will attack you. Don't fill your literature with responses to their attacks. You'll look weak. Stay positive and on the offensive. Keep responses to their attacks short.

In one local, officials accused an opponent of siding with management in a disciplinary case, a very serious accusation. The team knew they had to respond. They gave a clear factual account of what really happened and moved on.

Don't be too wordy. Members will not read long, complicated campaign literature. Keep it brief and to the point. A good rule of thumb—keep all your paragraphs to four lines or less.

Don't talk inside baseball. Focus on the critical issues facing members—not unfamiliar debates about the wording of bylaws or union process. Don't use campaign literature to address individual gripes or arguments. Remember, this literature is for the members, not for you.

YOUR PLATFORM

How do you get members to pay attention to your platform for change?

"When we first started talking to people, they said, 'It's not going to make a difference,'" said Walter Taylor, a long-time reformer in Teamsters Local 814 in New York, now a rep in the local.

"So we got specific. We told members how we were going to fight to win back our medical benefits, get pension contributions for casuals, and save 25-and-out retirement. That gave members a hope that we could make a real change. After we won, we stuck to our reform agenda and actually accomplished those things."

Be specific. Talk about *how* you will achieve results—not just the general goal you hope to achieve. Planks like "Start a steward training program," "Implement a grievant's bill of rights," and "Require union reps to visit worksites each morning" are all better than "Improve representation."

Focus on the workplace. Most members are concerned about what you can do to make work better. They're less likely to care about changes you'll make to union meetings and procedures—you'll need to show why those changes would matter.

Don't make promises you can't keep. If your local or your contract is in serious trouble, it won't be easy to turn around quickly. Instead talk about steps you will take to shift direction and start making improvements for the long term.

DEALING WITH ATTACKS

"You can count on the other side to attack you," warns Leonard Stoehr, recording secretary of Teamsters Local 728 in Atlanta. "You need to be smart in how you respond."

Here are some things to think about in planning your response:

Do you need to respond? The other side wants to put you on the defensive. You don't have to respond to every attack. Sometimes the best reaction is no reaction.

Warn your supporters that the other side will probably go negative. Other members will ask your supporters if the attacks are true. Give your supporters the facts so they can answer members' questions.

"Our opponents put out an anonymous flyer that asked 25 leading questions about our slate and our record," Stoehr said. "It was full of innuendos.

"We didn't put out an official response. But we talked to members of our team, so that we were all ready to respond when members asked us questions about the other side's attack."

Stoehr says when you get hit with an anonymous attack, point it out—it will make the attack look less serious.

Keep talking about your issues. Your opponents want you talking about their issues, not yours. If you need to respond, do it decisively, then move on.

"When we did respond, we always kept our responses short, factual, and to the point. That way we stayed on the offense," Stoehr says.

Warning: Don't let your lit do the talking. Good literature starts conversations, gets members talking about the issues, and makes a strong impression. Professional-looking literature shows you are serious and organized.

But many candidates make the mistake of thinking that good literature can do your campaigning for you. Good lit is a tool to help you talk to members. It's not a substitute.

[Adapted from *Running for Local Union Office*, which is available from Teamsters for a Democratic Union at www.tdu.org/rfo.]

LAYING THE GROUNDWORK BEFORE YOU RUN

by Chris Kutalik

Your mother might have been right about that old "try-and-try-until-you-succeed" saw. That certainly was the case for the victory of Teamsters (IBT) reformers at Local 743 in Chicago.

The New Leadership Slate swept to victory over the incumbents in 2007. It was the fourth election in over a decade's time in which Teamsters for a Democratic Union-affiliated reformers had tried to oust the old guard in the 12,000-member local.

TDU reformers pulled together the victorious slate after Local 743 officers were indicted by federal prosecutors in September 2007.

Since first launching opposition efforts more than a decade and a half ago, dissidents in the local had been fired, beaten up, and forced to watch as previous officer election victories were tossed out. But supporters of the reformers don't focus on making this a simple morality tale about keeping your chin up until you win.

A union election should be seen as one moment in a long campaign to change the union.

Instead, they talk about how building durable rank-and-file organization and leading workplace fights years before an election can pay off in the end.

ORGANIZATION THAT LASTS

Running for office, ironically enough, is not where budding reformers should start when running for office. The longtime reform group TDU counsels in its popular book *Running for Local Union Office* to look at elections as one moment in a long campaign to push bottom-up change in a union.

Defeats typically far outweigh victories for opposition activists. Success often hinges on growing a wide range of activist-leaders and keeping that organized core active for several years.

Richard Berg, the reformer who was elected president of Local 743, started his long trip in the local in 1988 as a freshly hired janitor at the University of Chicago hospital.

"We tried to get the fighters together first," Berg said. "A core of people at the local were inspired by [reform Teamster president] Ron Carey's win in 1991. We began trying to organize against a union leadership we saw as collaborating with the boss and deeply involved with corruption."

That initial core in the early 1990s was tiny, eight to 15 active participants, mostly from the university hospitals. But the fledgling group laid a foundation for long-term organization in those early years. Through careful outreach efforts they looked for leaders in isolated shop floor fights and tried to bring them into the group.

They also plugged into national networks such as TDU, the Association for Union Democracy, and Labor Notes both to help bolster morale and to build an external base of support. Equally as important, they looked to help train larger and larger groups of caucus members in the range of organizing skills they would need.

BUILDING OUTWARDS

A major challenge for any reform campaign in a large local is gaining sufficient strength in enough of the local's many worksites, units, and shifts that your group becomes truly representative of the union's rank and file. Local 743 nimbly vaulted this hurdle.

With upwards of 38,000 members until the 1980s, Local 743 was for years the largest local in the Teamsters. Though it has shrunk rapidly over the last decade, the local has retained a sprawling legacy. It covers more than 100 contracts spanning many small shops in a range of industries from nursing homes to light manufacturing plants to clerical staff in the IBT's own Central States Pension Fund.

The reformers in their early years took the step of exploring their union. They collected information on the contracts, work conditions, and workers. They attended meetings, visited work sites, and got involved in individual grievances to develop a grounded sense of how the union was supposed to function—and how it was really functioning.

The approach helped gird them for other obstacles. Not only was the local spread out among a bewildering array of shops, but it also had a broad range of ethnic groups who spoke a number of languages.

> **IF YOU ARE GOING TO TRY THIS AT HOME...**
>
> Winning office—and staying true to your principles and goals—is a difficult task in an era overshadowed by the declining strength of unions.
>
> While both creating long-term organization and leading from the shop floor are vital elements in a successful electoral drive, there are many other vital lessons to be remembered: starting early, creating a slate, developing a platform, planning ahead, and more.
>
> For a longer treatment of these lessons, see TDU's *Running for Local Union Office* book and Chapter 18, "Reform Caucuses and Running For Office," in *A Troublemaker's Handbook 2*.

They recruited into their caucus fluent speakers who could create flyers and newsletters and speak in workers' languages.

The reformers found that reaching out to workers took years of effort. Continuing corruption and decline in the union helped to push along their message.

Bob Simpson, Local 743's president at the time, was removed from office for corruption in 1995 by the Carey-run International. During the trusteeship the small reformer caucus spread quickly. Three years later, the reformers decided to put up a slate of their own in local elections. The New Leadership Slate was forged out of this organizing. Though they lost the election hands down, it gave them a much higher level of visibility.

LEAD FROM THE WORKPLACE

The new visibility in turn helped them not only to reach out to more members; it also put them increasingly into the role of the "go-to" people when rank and filers needed to wage a fight, according to Berg.

Many opportunities arose. When retail giant Montgomery Ward shut its doors in 2001 after a prolonged financial crisis, Local 743's biggest warehouse unit closed. Local leaders made no move to negotiate severance for workers, who turned to reformer activists to help them.

They organized large rallies and picketed the local's offices after local leaders refused their demand to bring the International in to help pressure a settlement with the retailer.

The caucus also took a leading role in a 2004 fight at Silver Capital, a small mirror and frame manufacturer in Bedford Park, a suburb of Chicago. The company had announced that it would be closing the plant and offered 150 workers little to no severance. Local leaders again made no move to oppose the closure plan.

Reform activists with ties to workers in the shop did, however. They set up pickets and shut the factory down.

While neither fight produced immediate gains for workers, it helped them build for a third, more successful workplace-closure fight at Fredrick Cooper's lamp factory on the northwest side of Chicago in 2005. Tony Caldera, a worker at the plant and an early caucus supporter, helped battle for severance pay.

The workers tapped support from community organizers who brokered leverage from sympathetic city aldermen. Ultimately they raised the temperature enough to win hundreds of thousands of dollars in severance pay.

HARD TEST

Local 743's reformers face the hard test of actually having to lead from office. Members are expecting them to make good on their reform platform.

"In the short run, we need to clean up the local's finances and sever all ties to the mob," said Berg. "In the long run, we need to involve the members and go beyond the normal routine of collective bargaining behind closed doors. We're committed to one-on-one member organizing."

Postscript: After Berg took office, he cut his salary by $70,000 and chopped officer salaries and staff. But some officers who ran on the reform ticket objected to having their salaries cut, and defended union reps who blew off grievance and arbitration responsibilities. The disgruntled officers filed internal union charges, saying Berg and Secretary-Treasurer Gina Alvarez had improperly settled a dispute with the union about a discharged employee's severance. Teamsters President James Hoffa removed them from office and suspended their membership. Sadly, the reform program stalled.

AVOIDING THE MISSTEPS NEW OFFICERS MAKE

by Dan Campbell

A lot of attention is paid to how new officers elected on a platform of reforming the union and mobilizing the members should run the local.

In the interest of fairness to the administrations that have gone very wrong, here is the other side of the story.

Put these suggestions to work for you and it's guaranteed: you'll have no problem coming in dead last in your next election. These not-too-carefully guarded secrets have been tried and tested by many well-meaning former leaders.

SELL OUT TO THE EMPLOYERS

Life will be so much easier. Make side deals. When you get tossed out of office, at least you'll have a few employer friends to call.

Every little compromise or concession you give leads to the dark side. Avoid meeting with employers without a steward or member present. Ban the "sidebar" unless you do it with members present or with the knowledge and consent of the members, which should include a detailed report.

FAIL TO PLAN

Who needs planning? Run from one crisis to the next.

You may be great at dodging icebergs, but why not make a plan to sail a little further south and avoid them altogether? Make planning a priority over all else. Get someone from outside to help, because you'll be too busy with day-to-day tasks. Someone from outside will bring perspective and tell you things you don't want to hear.

Do a big planning event once a year with your staff and key supporters. Then put someone in charge of scheduling check-up meetings three or four times a year.

NEVER LEAVE THE OFFICE

Tell the members you're at the office every day from sun-up to sundown. Fool yourself into thinking that's what they want.

You know the members' complaint: "We never see anyone from the hall unless there's an election." Make shop visits a top priority. Make a schedule to visit all your workplaces. Call supporters and let them know you're coming so they can prepare the members and meet you at the entrance. When you arrive (on time), don't visit the boss first.

Do cookouts in the parking lot or bring a cooler of cold drinks. You won't need much of an election campaign next time because you will have been on a nonstop campaign simply by doing your job.

TRY TO DO IT ALL

Members want you to personally take care of their problems, so tell them you will. When they call you again, tell them you're working on it. Or have your receptionist say you're in a meeting.

Unless you're in a very small local, don't try to be everyone's business agent. When you talk to members, listen, take notes, ask questions, and hear them out. Try to find areas of agreement. Don't debate, listen. Tell the member you will see that his or her concern is looked into by the appropriate person. Ask them to call you if they're not satisfied with what's being done. Assign the task and ask to be informed of progress and outcome. Members will not respect your staff if you don't.

NEGLECT YOUR BOARD

You only have to see them once a month. They'll surely go along with whatever you want even if you don't keep them informed. If they get out of line, denounce them as disloyal.

Communicate, consult, and delegate tasks to e-board members. In the case of a split e-board where you hold a majority, conduct a meeting with your supporters ahead of the regular meeting. Discuss upcoming business and informally decide how it will go. Then do your meeting. Give the opposition their right to speak on all items, take the vote, and move on.

If you have a split e-board where you're in a minority, focus on the most reasonable opposition members. Win them over to your program. If it's not possible, go to the members. Organize for the membership meetings and pass your program over their objections. Put the opposition board members on the defensive.

RUN A BAD MEETING

Your opposition is going to ask embarrassing questions and wait for you to make mistakes at meetings. Don't disappoint them. Wing it!

Prepare for membership meetings by scripting various parts. Stick to the script until you're comfortable working from an outline. Prepare your supporters in advance of meetings.

Build attendance by changing meeting times and places. Distribute flyers to generate interest in the topics to be discussed or special guests attending. Cut down on boring reports.

Serve food and beverages. Offer short educational programs. Show videos. Invite guests to report on victories. Give informative handouts and occasionally give door prizes.

NEGLECT YOUR OFFICE STAFF

These people work for you. Tell them you want them seen but not heard.

These staffers can make or break you. If the members get a crabby reception, no help with their problem, cut off, or put off, you're in major trouble. Special care must come especially from your health, welfare, and pension people. If members don't feel taken care of in this area, you get the blame.

Establish a policy for office staff: when a member has a problem, look for ways to be on their side instead of focusing on areas where you disagree.

DON'T HIRE GOOD STAFF

Hire your relatives. Or better yet, hire your opposition. Tell yourself that will make them loyal to you.

There are four criteria for hiring staff.

1) Loyalty to the reform movement along with demonstrated actions.

2) Loyalty to the reform movement along with demonstrated actions.

3) Loyalty to the reform movement along with demonstrated actions.

4) Competence.

Loyalty is defined as loyalty to the members and the reform program.

HAVE AN OPEN-DOOR POLICY

This is how you establish trust—by letting members visit you at their convenience.

The ideal is to give members adequate but not unlimited access. If you have a total open-door policy, you will find yourself reacting to situations rather than leading and working on priorities that will benefit all your members. It's akin to operating without a plan.

There is no substitute for a good secretary and a voicemail system that lets you control when to respond to your calls.

DON'T CONVERT TO THE MOBILIZING MODEL

Run the local the same way it's always been.

The members didn't elect you to be simply a more honest, cheaper, harder-working version of the group you replaced. The mobilizing model is the key to success, so bring the members into the game. Get help with this.

[For more detail on beginning a new union administration or refreshing an old one, including checklists, a stewards survey, and an assignment sheet, see chapter 6 of *Democracy Is Power.*]

Chapter Four

COMMUNICATING WITH MEMBERS AND THE PUBLIC

WINNING THE P.R. WAR IN A CONTRACT CAMPAIGN

by Randy Robinson

With my union—the Ontario Public Service Employees Union—under attack from a privatizing provincial premier in 1997, I didn't pay much attention to the strike by 185,000 U.S. Teamsters at UPS.

But more than a decade later, the two-week UPS strike (whose slogan was "Part-Time America Doesn't Work") was to have a profound effect on 6,000 workers at the Liquor Control Board of Ontario, the publicly owned agency that is the largest buyer of booze in the world, with revenues of almost $5 billion a year.

LCBO workers had taken their kicks. Under threat of privatization for years, they had agreed to several concessions, including low-paid casuals and a four-tier wage structure. New casuals would never reach the top of the pay grid, a difference of $2.15 an hour.

Those were tough times. But a few years later, Ontario had a new premier and LCBO workers had a new union. It was time for a different approach.

CAMPAIGN MANUAL

As we prepared for the 2008 contract showdown, I remembered hearing a presentation from Rand Wilson, who had run communications for the Teamsters in 1997. That memory brought me to discover *Outside the Box*, by Deepa Kumar.

Kumar's book told how UPS workers were 60 percent part-time with no benefits and with pay less than half the full-timers' hourly wage—same as at the LCBO. UPS workers had to lift things all day long, and it took a toll on their bodies—same as at the LCBO. UPS was immensely profitable, too—just like the LCBO.

Kumar told how a union on strike had won a public relations war in the mainstream media. We wanted to do that, too.

We bought 100 copies of Kumar's book. We gave it to our bargaining team, our member mobilizers, and the executive board. And we studied its lessons, namely that:

Big media is corporate, but by putting members in motion, the union can inject labor's concerns into the mainstream.

The mainstream media are corporations that fundamentally support what corporations do, but the tension between corporate ideology and the liberal idea of the free press can create spaces where a progressive message can take root.

No union can expect to attract media coverage without mobilizing members to take action.

Working people seldom hear about their concerns or their reality in the news, but when they do, it resonates. That can turn into real support for workers taking action.

The Teamsters' big issue at UPS was part-time jobs. The problem, skilfully articulated by the late Teamsters' President Ron Carey, was that low-wage jobs did not allow workers to live decently, raise their kids, or retire with dignity.

We took Carey's language and applied it directly to the Ontario situation.

TALK LIKE RON CAREY

As momentum built for the "Our communities need good jobs" campaign, OPSEU brought 100 union members to Toronto for training. We emphasized internal mobilizing and direct communication with the public in LCBO stores. We wanted every mobilizer to go home talking like Ron Carey. And they did.

The union controlled the message as the strike deadline loomed. Any reporter who asked, "What is this round of bargaining about?" did not hear about wages, benefits, or boot allowances.

They heard: "With a recession on, our communities need good jobs more than ever," said bargaining team chair Vanda Klumper. "Do we want an Ontario with good, permanent jobs with decent pay and benefits so regular people can live decently? Or will we accept disposable jobs that don't offer any hope for the future?"

We also created a way for union supporters to start conversations with LCBO workers. Campaigns Officer Sarah Jordison created "Booze Bucks," pieces of paper that looked like money and carried a message of support for the workers. The union handed more than 100,000 of these out to our other members, who in turn handed them to LCBO customer service reps in stores. They could literally see support walking in the door!

The bargaining unit is scattered in several hundred stores, warehouses, and offices around the province. The campaign was held together by a weekly newsletter and a strong web presence.

When members wore stickers on sticker day and buttons on button day, we took pictures and published them so members could see the momentum building. Twenty member mobilizers—booked off from work—took the union's message into workplaces and delivered it face to face.

Members reported back that the public was on our side.

"Usually when we set a strike deadline our customers tell us we should feel lucky to have jobs," one member said. "This time they're saying, 'Go for it.'"

Even the most reactionary of right-wing talk-radio hosts could not deny that people needed good jobs. And because the union was threatening the supply of that vital substance—liquor—no news outlet could ignore the story.

WHO BLINKS FIRST?

As the clock ticked down, the LCBO blinked.

In the final day of bargaining, the employer dropped all demands for concessions and the union made 30 different gains. Newer casuals won the right to get to the top of the pay grid, older workers won prescription-drug and dental benefits, and "fixed-term" casuals got a 15 percent pay hike on top of a wage increase. And the LCBO agreed to create more full-time jobs as well.

"Working people today are hungry for leadership that will lead them out of this mess," said OPSEU President Warren (Smokey) Thomas. "We told the public that good jobs—not corporate profits—are the bedrock of our economy, and the majority of the public said, 'You know, those crazy union people are right!'"

BOOST ORGANIZING WITH SOCIAL MEDIA

by Paul Abowd

Online social media tools like Twitter are often dismissed as time-wasters for the procrastinator in all of us. But they're also being harnessed for greater causes. You can use Twitter and text messaging to keep members educated, mobilize them for action, and empower worker-activists to shape the storyline of a campaign.

Twitter is a "micro-blogging" website that allows you to post frequent, short messages, using your computer or cell phone, to be read by people who've signed up to get your entries via their own computer or phone. Here are examples from four campaigns.

TWITTER ARMY

The Caucus of Rank and File Educators (CORE) formed in 2008 to push the Chicago Teachers Union to oppose school closings and fight for its members. According to spokesman Kenzo Shibata, the union had an "immense communications capacity which lay dormant when it was sorely needed."

As the city prepared to close yet more schools in 2009, Shibata says, the union was doing little to mobilize members. CORE's communication committee deployed a "Twitter army" to monitor major goings-on in the Chicago education world.

The group began sending live tweets from the union's monthly House of Delegates meetings. The gatherings were sparsely attended by non-delegates but decided on issues that affected all members. Now everyone could keep tabs on how their dues were spent.

The Twitter brigade also descended on monthly Board of Education meetings, which are held during the work day, making it difficult for teachers and students to get out. Shibata says CORE sent "quick

> **New forms of communication can pull members closer to the union and spur action.**

bursts of analysis" to teachers, who read up during their lunch breaks.

When Secretary of Education Arne Duncan returned to Chicago for a speaking engagement sponsored by a pro-privatization group, CORE activists picketed outside and reported via Twitter that they had been threatened with arrest for trying to enter. A flood of teachers responded with solidarity messages, and others asked for directions to the protest.

TEXT TO WIN

In summer 2008 Teamsters at Sotheby's, the art auction house in New York, won their best contract in a decade. The campaign was helped along by a text-message phone tree, which members set up to connect the workforce of 50. Sotheby's workers are continually moving from one part of their 10-story building to another and some are out and about on deliveries.

Rank and filer Julian Tysh says the shop's organizing committee set up the text network after discovering that workers young and old were punching out texts on their cell phones. "We started using it to get people to show up for impromptu meetings: hurry up and meet outside, the bargaining committee is going to give you an update on how things are going," he said. "We'd meet on the street in front of the building or on the loading dock." Seventy to 80 percent showed up at the impromptu report-backs.

When the campaign began to escalate, says Tysh, designated texters might send messages asking workers to wear a union shirt the next day and gather at the time clock 20 minutes early.

TEXTS ON THE DOCKS

Texting brought together far-flung longshore activists in a yearlong contract campaign stretching across dozens of ports from Maine to Texas.

The Longshore Workers Coalition, a reform group inside the East Coast Longshoremen's (ILA) union, used texting to reach hundreds of new recruits, quickly disseminate bargaining updates about concessions union leaders had accepted in secret backroom meetings, and organize a September 2009 contract rejection that sent the deal back for improvement.

Texting is an organizer's new best friend, says LWC staffer Marsha Niemeijer. After learning to ask for cellphone numbers, she added new people automatically to the text list (and diligently removed those who wanted off). Receiving messages gives a recruit an identification with the organization. From there an organizer can use the connection to have a conversation with the potential member and build a deeper relationship.

"Besides an information tool, it's an action tool," Niemeijer said, noting that she tailored texts to specific ports or groups of activists, inviting members to distribute flyers and join rallies.

In a union culture where members get little information and meetings are poorly attended, the LWC's texts became must-have items at contract time. In Norfolk, Virginia, signs went up on the local's wall with the number to subscribe. One Baltimore member called the message system "our CNN."

About 90 percent of the LWC membership is on the text list now, up from 60 percent before the campaign. (Email doesn't work among a computer-phobic membership, Niemeijer said.)

How much is too much? At its peak, the LWC blasted out three messages a day, several days a week. Niemeijer said she can count the number of negative reactions on one hand.

"It's not a replacement for the human connection, but it increases our chances of getting people to be part of something larger," Niemeijer said. "It adds a level of excitement, and members feel good about being in the know."

FROM PHONE TO NET

In Southern California, a digital storytelling and community journalism project built by students and low-wage workers gives recent immigrants without computers a connection to the digital world by using low-cost new media.

The project developed software that allows workers to use their phones to capture and publish pictures, videos, and stories about their jobs, families, and activism.

The "Mobile Voices" program, or "Vozmob," exists primarily for day laborers and domestic workers, said Sasha Costanza, a board member.

Workers who weren't cell-phone-savvy before are now editing their own videos and sharing their knowledge at worker-to-worker trainings throughout L.A. The software for uploading stories to the web can be downloaded free at www.vozmob.net, and works on any basic cell phone, including the low-cost, prepaid phones used by many immigrant workers. Workers send their dispatches by phone to an email address, which directly uploads the messages to Vozmob's blog.

A project of the L.A.-based Instituto de Educacion Popular del Sur de California and the University of Southern California, Vozmob has been used by workers to cover a community health conference, job centers and day laborers' issues, and student organizing against tuition hikes.

At a National Domestic Workers Alliance conference in the Bay Area, a Vozmob member who blogs as "Madelou" trained other domestic workers how to use the technology. Madelou took pictures of the spirited march for domestic workers' rights and sent updates throughout the conference from her phone to the blog.

Constanza says workers are also using this technology to document their workplace problems online with pictures, text, and audio—a great way to catalog evidence for grievances.

WHEN YOUR BOSS DOESN'T 'LIKE' YOU: SURVIVING IN SOCIAL MEDIA

by Mischa Gaus

Social media are presenting new challenges for unions as employers develop policies and discipline employees for their posts on Facebook, Twitter, and YouTube.

But whether workers are talking to each other in the lunch room or online, labor law still provides protections for private-sector workers to engage in concerted activities with their co-workers.

Salty language and sarcasm doesn't necessarily disqualify a post from legal protections.

The National Labor Relations Board has reviewed more than 100 cases involving social media and has upheld these rights. It has struck down several employer policies that interfere with workers' protections when they're online.

If your employer wants to introduce a policy for social media, he must provide the union a meaningful opportunity to bargain. That gives a smart union time to discover the potential impact of the policy, and get members involved in a campaign to protect their rights.

LAW IS STILL THE LAW

The NLRB issued a memo in August 2011 spelling out its guidelines for social media policies, which we're summarizing here.

If your members are disciplined over their behavior on social media, as their steward you should handle it like any other disciplinary action. Start by determining what social media post got your member disciplined.

Any communication by a worker (spoken or written) that

was protected before Facebook is still protected. These messages have to be among co-workers and relate to the "terms and conditions" of employment: workload, job performance, wage issues, staffing levels.

In one case, a domestic violence advocate at a nonprofit agency repeatedly texted and asked co-workers on Facebook whether employees were doing enough to assist clients. Four co-workers responded on Facebook and all five were fired. The NLRB upheld the workers' rights, calling it a "textbook example of concerted activity."

Protesting supervisory actions is protected, too, but the complaint can't be an individual gripe. The board has said the post should indicate that the worker wants to "initiate or induce co-workers to engage in group action." A combination of offline and online conversation can show the worker is encouraging co-workers to share her position—which is protected activity.

Salty language and sarcasm don't necessarily disqualify the communication from labor law protections. One worker was fired after calling her supervisor a "scumbag" on Facebook, but the board ordered her rehired because her comment came during a discussion with co-workers that occurred outside the workplace during nonwork time, and because the posting didn't interrupt work.

On the other hand, the board did not protect a bartender upset over a new tipping policy who called his customers "rednecks" and said he hoped they would choke on glass. He made the comment to a relative, and there was no evidence he had brought up his concerns about pay with any co-worker.

Posts that violate an employer's privacy policy, disparage the employer or its products, or are "so disloyal, reckless, or maliciously false" as to lose the law's protection can be disciplined. Employees in the health care field must also be careful not to violate patient privacy protections online.

ELECTRONIC BIRDY TOLD ME

Sometimes how the employer discovers the post can be a good defense. It's unlawful for a boss to threaten, interrogate, or engage in surveillance of employees' social media behavior, if the communications are relevant to the conditions of employment.

However, if the employer received the union member's social media post, unsolicited, from one of the member's "friends," the employer has not engaged in unlawful surveillance.

Companies are rushing to establish their social media policies. The NLRB has said many employers' policies are so overly broad that "employees could reasonably construe them to prohibit protected conduct." These include policies that ban "embarrassing the employer" or "damaging goodwill" or that prohibit workers from "disclosing inappropriate or sensitive information."

The board overturned these polices because the language was so expansive it could bar co-workers from finding each other online, taking photos of the company logo during a protest, or discussing the company's treatment of workers.

BE PREPARED TO BARGAIN

If your employer wants to establish a policy, he must bargain with the union about it. And if he has already adopted a policy and didn't notify the union, that's an unfair labor practice.

But many discipline proceedings and NLRB charges could be avoided if the unions involved had demanded bargaining, and effectively bargained, when these policies were first introduced. Under the National Labor Relations Act, as well as under many state labor laws, the employer is required to give notice to the union of any change in policy that would impact the conditions of employment.

If your employer wants to establish a policy, he must bargain with the union about it.

The employer is further required to provide an opportunity to bargain. This means that telling the union that a policy is going into effect the next day would be considered an unfair labor practice. These rights mean very little unless the union is prepared to take action, however. Critical steps include:

- Putting in an immediate demand to bargain
- Submitting information requests about the proposed policy, about its purpose, about who was involved in creating the policy, and about its proposed application, extent, and scope
- Communicating with members about the proposed policy, its potential impacts, and the union's activities around the policy
- And building a member-involving campaign to support the union's bargaining position.

If social media is to be a tool for collective action, our rights to use it must be aggressively protected.

[Thanks to the United Electrical Workers and Charley Richardson for providing elements of this article.]

USING THE AIRWAVES TO EDUCATE AND MOBILIZE WORKERS

by Tiffany Ten Eyck

If you happen to be scanning the radio dial near two unique towns in the United States, you could stumble across something unusual: FM radio run by and for farmworkers. In Woodburn, Oregon, and south central Florida, farmworkers have added low-power community radio to their organizing arsenal.

Worker centers use the radio stations to educate and mobilize workers to fight for better wages, dignity on the job, and immigrant rights.

To set up their radio stations, the two organizations—Oregon's Northwest Treeplanters and Farmworkers United (PCUN) and Florida's Coalition of Immokalee Workers (CIW)—called on the Prometheus Radio Project.

A radio station celebrates members' culture and becomes an essential training tool.

The non-profit helps low-wage communities set up radio stations and learn the technical aspects of keeping a radio station alive.

POWERED BY WORKERS

Called "low-power" radio because the signal does not travel as far as commercial outlets, the stations target the communities they serve, with a range of five to seven miles.

Radio activists with Prometheus say the name can be a problem as the stations are hardly low on people power.

Radio Movimiento (Movement Radio) in Oregon and Radio Consciencia (Consciousness Radio) in Florida are built on these two namesake principles: building a stronger farmworker movement while raising the consciousness of farmworkers and the community that surrounds them. Dozens of recent immigrants and farmworkers have been trained as radio DJs and technicians.

"Our radio station is led by a volunteer committee of farmworkers that keep the talk shows and call-in shows going," said Gerardo Reyes Chavez, a member of the CIW who hosts shows on Radio Consciencia each evening. "People call in during breaks or when they aren't able to find work in the fields, and they request their favorite songs."

While Radio Consciencia prides itself on playing the *norteñas, bachatas,* and other popular Spanish or indigenous language music their listeners want to hear, the real goal is to educate the farmworker community about the organization's work to raise wages and improve working conditions in Florida fields.

The CIW has already been successful in getting 10 major food corporations to meet its demand for a penny more per pound paid to tomato pickers. "We promote the campaign for fair food to the community, especially to the new immigrants, and share announcements about upcoming actions and protests and invite the community to sign up at the CIW office to join us," Reyes said.

"There are different levels of consciousness in the community and the messages in the radio are seeds being planted in those that listen—they're the first steps of consciousness," Reyes said. "Our work on the ground is the next step, visiting people in their homes, inviting them to our weekly meetings and strategy meetings."

MOBILIZING TOOL

Radio Movimiento started broadcasting in August 2006, becoming the first union in Oregon to have a radio station. PCUN, like many commercial radio stations that cater to Latino immigrants, used the radio to promote participation in May Day immigrant rights marches. PCUN reported that the May 1 immigrants rights rally at the state capital in Salem drew 5,000, twice what they expected. They credit radio.

When workers run a radio station, their ability to update other workers about potential threats increases. When workers at Fresh Del Monte, a fruit and vegetable processing company in Portland, were faced with a raid by Immigration and Customs Enforcement, Radio Movimiento broadcast call-in reports from the scene, and updated the community about false reports of other ICE activity in the area.

In Immokalee, workers use the station to build their campaigns.

"Every week, we go to the camps where farmworkers live with a sound system and broadcast live while passing out flyers encouraging our fellow workers to participate," Reyes said.

RADIO THAT PAYS

"The radio has been really effective against many types of abuses, like non-payment," Reyes said. "We use the station to talk about what to do when a boss or crew leader refuses to pay somebody."

After Hurricane Charley hit in 2004, one construction company that came to Immokalee hired around 600 people to help in the cleaning and rebuilding effort. A group of workers came to the CIW's office and told organizers they hadn't received pay—some for a week, others for a month.

"We decided to make an announcement and put it on the radio that asked workers who had worked on the rebuilding after the hurricane but hadn't been paid to come to the CIW office," Reyes said. "We thought there would be a slow trickle in, but after only two hours, 200 workers were standing outside the office. We realized the problem was bigger than we thought—and that people were listening to the radio.

"We contacted the company and they offered to sit down with us and work out a solution. About 300 workers total ended up receiving the pay that they were owed."

RAPID RESPONSE

Radio in farmworker communities is an example of a good organizing strategy whose impact extends past the immediate campaign for workers' rights. In communities that are under-resourced, workers at the helm of mass communication can provide resources and help that are otherwise absent.

When Hurricane Wilma was bearing down on Immokalee in October 2005, CIW organizers were concerned. The majority of farmworkers in the area live in trailers that would not withstand a hurricane. Workers responded to the threat by looping an emergency announcement on the radio informing the community where they could find safe shelter.

CIW organizers began transporting farmworkers, who didn't own cars. Reyes said that in a situation like this radio saved lives: "When we returned the next day, the roof of one of the housing complexes that we had helped evacuate had fallen in."

PCUN and CIW have been successful with low-power radio not only because their members and supporters have become involved in the daily running of the stations, but also because the stations meet the needs of their members. "Not every person has a TV," Reyes said. "But they have a radio."

[For more information about Prometheus Radio, go to prometheusradio.org. For more information about PCUN go to www.pcun.org. For more information on the CIW, go to www.ciw-online.org.]

PUTTING LABOR FILMS TO WORK

by Chris Garlock and Jon Garlock

Hey, organizers, let's put on a show!

Workers are using video to document and share their struggles, and filmmakers from every corner of the globe are addressing labor themes.

Labor film festivals are emerging: 2009 saw no less than 14 screenings, from Montana to Dublin, Ireland, and from Cape Town, South Africa, to South Charleston, West Virginia.

The timing is right for films about work and workers. Plus, everyone loves movies. They have an amazing power to bring people together, whether it's lesbian activists mingling with straight union members at "Live Girls Unite!", about an organizing drive at a San Francisco

"The Philosopher Kings," 2009.

strip club, or classical music fans rubbing shoulders with Liszt-loving hard hats at "Note By Note," the story of the year-long making of a Steinway piano.

As longtime labor film organizers in Washington, D.C., and Rochester, New York, we've been inspired by the surge of interest in organizing local film events.

A movie series brings labor's values to a wide audience.

Throughout the year, activists stop us on picket lines to ask when the next film is or to suggest one to show. Sometimes they just want to share the impact that a film made on their lives. Often we hear that seeing a labor film helped a spouse, family member, or friend "to finally understand what I do."

Viewing labor films as a group builds the solidarity of shared experience.

A festival that continues year after year builds a following, a community of moviegoers, friends, and sponsors who make the festival a regular feature of the cultural calendar.

Labor film events come in many sizes and formats. Here are some issues to consider:

AUDIENCE

Are you reaching out mainly to union members, to working people who may or may not have union cards, or to a mixed labor and general audience? One of the main advantages of a labor film event is to reach people who may not appreciate what unions actually are.

Our experience is that about a third of the audience will be union members, another third film buffs, and the rest a general audience attracted to the particular film. Over 20 years, nearly 20,000 have attended the screenings in Rochester, while better than 10,000 came to D.C.'s during the 2000s.

"Bound for Glory," 1976.

COORDINATION

Identify an organization and a lead individual to organize and sponsor the event. They will recruit partners and coordinate overall.

Central labor councils are a natural starting place, as in both D.C. and Rochester.

TYPE OF EVENT

Is this a single screening? A festival, like the annual D.C. Labor FilmFest, which shows nearly two dozen films over an entire week? A series, like Rochester's Labor Film Series, which screens one film a week over two months? Better to start small and grow your event over time.

"The Planning Lady," a 2007 short.

VENUE

Will your screenings be in a union hall, a commercial or "art" theater, a campus auditorium, a museum? We prefer existing film institutions—like our partners the George Eastman House in Rochester or the American Film Institute in D.C.—because they are experienced at film selection and acquisition and can guide you through the unfamiliar world of film. While it's possible to screen DVDs in a union hall, a movie theater is the best venue. They avoid copyright issues and bring in wider audiences.

FILM SELECTION

If you collaborate with a theater, you'll be working with a programmer to select 35mm or 16mm films. Programmers can advise on film titles and work with distributors to book films. You may find it helpful to recruit a team to preview and select films.

PUBLICITY

Outreach is just like getting folks to a labor rally: get the word out early and often. A good way to build the audience is to give sponsoring locals free or reduced-price tickets. Working with partner institutions can bring coverage from entertainment reporters and publications. Developing these relationships yourself can often help you to get improved coverage of other labor events in the future.

COSTS

Your budget will include film rental and shipping, film projection, and printing of promotional materials. Another strong incentive to partner with an existing film institution is that it will likely share most costs, since your program will bring in paying audiences. Both the Rochester and D.C. film events are funded through support from sponsors, mostly local unions.

Organizing a labor film event is easier than you think and can provide creative ways to build the labor movement in your community. It's a space where workers' issues and struggles can become visible once more. See you at the movies!

[See more at www.dclabor.org and www.rochesterlabor.org.]

Chapter Five

ORGANIZING FROM THE BOTTOM UP

BUILDING A STEWARDS COUNCIL

by Paul Krehbiel

Want a stronger union at work? Consider building a stewards council.

With only five stewards for 1,700 workers, demoralization was high at the Harbor-UCLA Medical Center in Los Angeles.

The union, the old Service Employees (SEIU) Local 660, was very weak there. Many members complained that the union did nothing, and they wanted out.

On-the-job structure gives members a powerful tool for collective action.

The only solution was to build the union at the facility. The most active stewards met and we came up with an assessment and a plan. We knew we couldn't handle every problem at the facility at once, so we decided to concentrate on one manageable work area of about 20-30 workers at a time. We used three key criteria to decide where to focus our efforts:

There needed to be a problem that affected most workers in the area. It needed to be a problem that people felt strongly about. Finally, we wanted to focus on areas where there was a leader or potential leader in the group.

SETTING GUIDELINES

Once we found such a group, we had three goals: (1) organize an issue campaign that would involve a significant majority, (2) try to win a victory, and (3) recruit at least one leader to become a steward. Our long-term goal was to have at least one steward in every work area, on every shift, in a ratio of at least one steward for every 20 workers.

Once we had recruited at least 12 stewards who were representative of the workforce in the different areas, we would set up an interim stewards council. When we had 20 stewards, we would establish the permanent stewards council.

The council would function as a democratic body—we would elect officers and write and approve a simple constitution, bylaws, and mission statement that mandated member input and democratic practices. All the while, we would need to keep recruiting.

BUILDING A CAMPAIGN

Two workers on the hospital's 4 West ward called the union, complaining that management had issued a memo stating that workers had to bring in a doctor's note if they took a sick day in December. The usual policy had required a doctor's note after three days off.

When stewards met with the callers, they said everyone was strongly opposed to this change. But we chose to circulate a petition to gauge the level of support. Doing so could teach leadership skills to signature gatherers.

Within three days, 23 of 25 workers signed. We decided to file a group grievance and have as many people come into the grievance meeting as possible.

The lead workers mapped their work area by making a list of all the workers there. They got 12 workers to agree to come and speak at the grievance meeting. They came in on their breaks, two at a time, every 15 minutes. It took an hour and a half, and work slowed down considerably.

Management was worried, and backed off on enforcing the new rule. Workers were happy and one leader became a steward.

We repeated this process in other work areas and within four months we formed the interim stewards council. Within eight months, we had built a permanent stewards council that had elected its own officers.

LEADERSHIP AND EDUCATION

The council put out letters and leaflets in its name, conducted larger campaigns at the facility, and was soon seen by workers and management as *the* union at the work site.

Internal education is essential for a strong, well-functioning stewards council. We decided to hold steward training classes early in the recruitment process. We held them after work at the hospital, once a week, to make it easy for stewards to attend. Regular classes covered the nuts and bolts of daily union action—grievances, communications, problem-solving. Others covered specific issues the union was building campaigns around.

Most of the classes emphasized looking for group issues, because fighting for a group would strengthen the union much more than fighting for just one person.

More experienced stewards took part in presenting a portion of a class, and the most advanced conducted a full class when they felt ready. One of our goals was to get the more experienced stewards to help train the less experienced ones.

We also set up a mentoring program. New stewards would accompany more experienced ones to meetings with management to see firsthand how issues were handled. As they gained knowledge, skills, and confidence, they began to participate more and more.

Our goal was to get as many stewards as possible to run meetings with co-workers and management by themselves. This gave the union a big boost.

MAKING YOUR EDUCATION RELEVANT

At a Los Angeles medical center, the Service Employees Local 660 stewards council decided they wanted member feedback before deciding what training to offer.

Each steward talked to co-workers and listed what kinds of information they thought would be most useful. Stewards brought the council's ideas back to members, too. "It doesn't make sense to hold classes if they aren't the things the members think are important," said one steward.

The feedback clearly said members wanted tools to deal with daily problems: how to investigate a grievance, how to write one, how to interview witnesses, how to prepare your case, and how to present it.

A number of workers also asked how to solve problems without filing a formal grievance, allowing us to introduce ideas of collective action into the classes, by discussing the big gains made at key times in labor history through mass marches, strikes, and other collective action.

Since we gave examples of how individual grievances with great merit were routinely denied by management, this led naturally to a class on organizing.

We used a workshop-type approach, with small group discussions, role plays, and skits. We also used real on-the-job problems in the classes. We made sure to get feedback at the end of a class with a quick evaluation form.

The classes accomplished our most important goal—to empower the stewards and raise their level of union consciousness. More stewards left with the skills and tools they needed to better handle problems on the job.

BRINGING PEOPLE IN

Soon, word was out that the union was alive and growing. Workers in other areas came to us, asking to become stewards. We asked them to help on a project and then brought them aboard.

Within a year and a half, we had 35 stewards and the union was winning some victories. Things were far from perfect, but management knew that the union was there.

Stewards councils make a big difference. When workers have one, they feel that *they* are the union—and that they have power.

A STRONG STEWARDS COUNCIL CAN WIN A BIG CAMPAIGN

by Paul Krehbiel

A Los Angeles medical center that employed 3,500 workers had been grappling with understaffing for years. It was particularly acute among nurses, who also protested the most.

How was the union going to tackle this huge issue?

The old Service Employees (SEIU) Local 660 already had a stewards council in place when I arrived as a staff rep. Among the 45 stewards, a half-dozen were experienced, another 15 would help, and the rest weren't very active.

When the union's reach is deep into the workplace, stewards can lead bold actions.

We needed more stewards, and they needed to be more involved. We wanted one steward for every 15 workers, so we had a considerable way to go.

At the same time, SEIU and other unions in California were trying to implement a new nurse-to-patient ratio law that they had worked for years to pass. In the Los Angeles County Department of Health Services, management had made no progress in reducing the number of patients assigned to nurses.

The law mandated no more than six patients per nurse on most wards. Nurses were routinely assigned 10, 15, or sometimes 20 patients. Nurses were angry and wanted action. We had meetings with management and were assured that they were working hard to hire new nurses and needed more time. Months went by with no improvement.

The staffing problem was a hot topic at stewards council meetings and the council supported the nurses. Stewards headed back to their work areas and talked about the importance of backing the nurses.

"We especially wanted stewards on patient care wards to talk to the nurses and other workers there," said Keenan Sheedy, co-chair of the stewards council and a patient financial services worker.

GATHERING INFORMATION

The stewards council set up a subcommittee, made up of nurses, other stewards, and union staff. "We began by researching the law," said Fred Huicochea, a utilization review nurse and shop steward. "We found a law that mandated nurses to ensure the safety of the patient. We told the nurses that they had the legal right under the Nurse Practice Act not to accept an unsafe patient assignment."

Stewards from the council, with the help of the union reps, went to all 22 wards in the hospital, on all three shifts, to tell nurses about this safe patient care law and their rights, and ask them if they wanted to participate in a campaign to refuse unsafe assignments.

Audrey Nwankwo, another nurse steward, said they handed out leaflets quoting the safe patient language exactly as it was written in the law.

When stewards and staff talked to the nurses on each ward, they kept notes, so that at the end, we knew which wards were the strongest. Ultimately, we chose four wards to start the "safe patient care campaign."

REFUSING UNSAFE ASSIGNMENTS

On the day we started the campaign, we explained that county management was in violation of both the new ratio law and the law that required nurses to ensure patient safety. Management was furious and threatened the nurses, telling them they would be insubordinate if they refused to take the number of patients assigned to them. The nurses immediately called us to their wards and we all argued with the managers.

Management called the police, who threatened to arrest us. When a manager told a nurse to take another patient—in front of the police—I said the manager was breaking the law and that I wanted the manager arrested. The police were dumbfounded and called their headquarters for instructions.

We stayed there for three hours until the hospital was in compliance. On some wards, management found additional nurses; on others they had to close beds and transfer the patients elsewhere.

SPREADING INFORMATION

That first day was a big success. The next day, council members and staff handed out leaflets announcing the victories of the courageous nurses on the four wards to nurses entering for their morning shift.

There was a buzz throughout the hospital. Nurses on other wards joined the campaign. Within five days the campaign had spread to 17 wards. Licensed Vocational Nurses, nursing attendants, and ward clerks spoke up, led by stewards from the council, saying that the additional patients assigned to the RNs caused *them* to have unsafe assignments, too, since they had to help the RNs.

Stewards from the council explained the laws to the nurses and what they should say to management. Management was stunned by the broad support for the campaign and the tenacity of the nurses not to back down in the face of repeated threats.

The stewards council put out an issue of its newsletter to all the workers in the hospital, explaining how the campaign was built and won, encouraging them to see they could do the same thing to address problems in their areas.

Nurses with 20 years or more said this campaign did more to improve working conditions than anything that had ever happened at the hospital.

HOW TO BREAK DOWN CRAFT DIVISIONS THROUGH A CAMPAIGN

by Paul Krehbiel

After Service Employees (SEIU) Local 660 members won a campaign to enforce safe staffing levels for registered nurses at a Los Angeles medical center, management was angry.

So they retaliated.

Rather than take on the nurses again, management targeted workers in classifications that they thought were weaker. They played on divisions between different types of workers.

The first wave was against licensed vocational nurses (LVNs), nursing attendants, and clerks, many of whom had supported the nurses' campaign.

Management thought it had singled out a weaker group of workers, but stewards got everyone to push back.

Management increased weekend work for these groups to three or more weekends a month. Nurses weren't affected because they had language in their contract giving them every other weekend off, and they had just demonstrated their strength. The other classifications didn't have that language in their contracts.

"We had been working hard to improve staffing to improve patient care, and it looked like management was trying to punish us by forcing us to work more weekends," said Sabrina Griffin, a LVN and co-chair of the stewards council.

Griffin brought the issue to the stewards council, which passed a resolution demanding that LVNs, attendants, and clerks get back their regular weekends off. Then they began organizing a campaign.

CAMPAIGN KICKOFF

The campaign started with a petition. Cynthia Molette, a transcriber typist and stewards council member, explained this would show management "just how many workers were opposed to the extra weekend work."

There was a high level of support. Quickly, more than 200 workers had signed the petitions. Copies were made for every ward, and at an agreed-upon date and time, delegations of workers on each ward delivered the petitions to their ward managers, while a larger delegation, organized by the stewards council, delivered the original petitions to nursing administration.

Administrators were stunned. They didn't expect the council to mobilize members on nearly all 22 wards of the hospital. They quickly gave in and reverted to the old weekend-off schedule.

But management didn't give up. They next singled out a smaller group of workers that they saw as politically weaker, the nurse attendants.

Normally, two attendants work a ward of 22-24 patients. Their duties include taking basic vital signs, changing bedsheets, cleaning up, giving baths, assisting nurses and LVNs, and transporting patients. When management pulled one attendant off each ward, doubling their workload, this caused serious problems. The attendants immediately brought the issue before the stewards council.

DIVIDING TO CONQUER

Many stewards felt that management targeted the attendants because they perceived them as the most vulnerable. They are overwhelmingly women and people of color. Many of them are immigrants, and they are also low-paid.

Reducing the number of attendants would have put pressure on the nurses to do the attendants' work. There was already a long historical divide between attendants and RNs, and these staffing cuts would pit the workers against each other.

The stewards council jumped to respond. With input and leadership from the attendants, the council put out a petition demanding that all patient care wards have two attendants. The petition also had a column for workers to put their job classification, to show broad support for the attendants.

The council organized a delegation of 10 workers from all classifications to meet with management.

"We all support the attendants," Joel Solis, an RN steward leader on the delegation, told the nursing director. "For the first time, the

RNs, LVNs, attendants, and clerks are supporting each other. This helps us all and ensures the best care for our patients."

Management agreed to put 26 attendants back on the wards. From RNs to attendants, it was clear to everyone that having a strong, permanent stewards council was the best safeguard against retaliation.

HOW TO INVOLVE YOUNG MEMBERS

by Tiffany Ten Eyck

When CAMI Automotive hired 500 new employees in Ingersoll, Ontario, many of the new folks were under 30 and starting their first union jobs.

The Canadian Auto Workers wanted to make sure new hires got involved in the union, so CAW Local 88 leaders came up with an inspired answer: start a youth committee. "If the committee was successful," said Local 88 President Cathy Austin, "the plan was to get a youth member-at-large on the union's executive board."

WINNING THE UNION OVER

Not everyone in the union was enthusiastic about the idea at first. "There was quite the debate on the floor," Austin said. "People asked, 'Why do they need a special committee? I never had a youth committee when I was young.'"

John Bridges, co-chair of the youth committee, said the logic behind supporting the committee was clear: "The importance of a youth committee is to engage younger members in the union. We all know that the working world is getting a lot older. If we don't fully engage the youth, who's going to protect the older workers' pensions?"

There's 1,000 ways to get new members engaged, but it won't happen on its own.

Once established, the committee thrived. "Eventually everyone recognized the energy the youth had," Austin said.

The election for the board seat improved their standing. Four people ran for the youth position. "They were so bright, articulate, and enthusiastic they won people over when campaigning," she said.

But even once the union agreed to the committee and a young person took a seat on the executive board, some union members voiced concerns about promoting young workers into leadership in a two-tier work environment. "One of the first things that was said was, 'Why send them to conferences? They're going to be gone at first layoff,'" Austin said. "But that's just asinine. If they do get laid off or leave, they're going into the workforce with all that union knowledge."

GETTING INVOLVED

The youth committee was unsure what it should be doing at first. Austin encouraged members to jump in wherever they wanted.

Many new hires worked the midnight shift (or "C shift") and lacked access to the union hall for socializing and interaction with the union. Bridges said they combated this by hosting an annual C shift breakfast "to get midnight people out to the hall."

Austin said that through the committee's organizing, solidarity was built between the youth committee and the retiree chapter. The two groups worked on a picnic together, giving young folks a chance to hear the stories of the retirees, like their strike of 1992.

Internal organizing doesn't happen on its own, Austin said.

"You need to give support and space to get it started and give young members wide latitude to decide what they're interested in doing," she said. "There's 1,000 ways to get involved in the union—let them find their way."

To get new ideas, the youth committee links up with similar committees across the CAW and compares notes. That's how youth committee members found out about a protest in support of Delphi workers at the Detroit Auto Show, which they attended.

Bridges said that to get young people involved in the union, they had to lead by example. New workers might be "afraid to get involved, but after seeing us going to meetings they want to get involved. We explain what's going to happen and they might go to the next meeting."

STRENGTHENING THE UNION

Austin reported that the youth committee has helped keep young people engaged in the union—and given the local a new way to reach its young members.

"It's an interesting and scary time in the union right now," she said. "Some unions are extending the amount of time needed to grow into full wages, and with two-tier wages, two-tier benefits, and two-tier pensions, young workers have a lot at stake right now. Without their voice in the union, it's a lose-lose situation for them and for us."

DEFEATING PRIVATIZATION

by David Cohen

"Why privatize? We can run it better!" That's the question asked by United Electrical Workers Local 274 and the Office and Professional Employees (OPEIU) when their wastewater treatment plant was threatened with privatization.

The city council—known as a Selectboard—in Montague, Massachusetts, a town of 8,500 in the western part of the state, was concerned about the treatment plant because it had lost a large industrial customer. But the Selectboard never thought to ask the people who worked there what to do.

People support public facilities that they think are well-run, so be prepared to make the case.

Instead, it solicited bids to privatize the plant, in hopes of saving the town money. Soon, four companies had handed in proposals, most of which promised big savings. Because of intense pressure from union members, none of the proposals called for layoffs or wage cuts (except, perhaps, cuts in management).

Montague has an unusual governance structure that allows for ample public input. Five elected Selectboard members meet weekly, and the town budget is voted on at representative town meetings of 150 people elected from precincts. The unions knew they had to take their case to the public.

PACK THE HOUSE

The Selectboard held public hearings on the proposal to privatize, and these hearings were broadcast live on the local cable TV station.

Union members made sure they packed the audience to hear the companies present their proposals on how they would run the facility.

But the companies never discussed how they would be paid. When the time came for questions, the unions immediately asked, "How much are you going to make for running the facility?"

After beating around the bush, the largest company answered that it would receive 10 percent of the operating budget as its "fee." Union members in the audience pointed out that this gave the companies the incentive to increase the budget instead of cutting costs.

Many of the Selectboard members thought that if the facility was privatized the company would assume all costs. Under intense questioning by the union, the companies admitted that the town would pay for repairs and replacement parts, such as generators and pumps.

This was the moment the unions were waiting for. They asked for time to create a proposal for more efficient ways to run the plant. The bosses, who had assured the Selectboard they had done everything possible to cut costs, were outraged.

But the Selectboard agreed, their faith in privatization shaken by the looming costs for repairs and the built-in fees.

THE UNION PLAN

For the next several weeks, the union members worked on their proposal. The only guideline: no wage, benefit, or job cuts. The workers voted to exclude management from the planning sessions because the plant manager was the person who had first proposed privatization.

Both UE members (who operated the plant) and OPEIU members (who handled the clerical work and laboratory testing) participated. Many of the proposals were ideas they had pushed management to try for many years. Workers made lists of their ideas, hashed through them in meetings, and threw away plenty.

The clerical workers wrote up the winning ideas in easy-to-understand language for the Selectboard and the public, who didn't fully comprehend how the facility worked.

The result was a detailed report calling for higher usage and earnings by processing waste from other communities, and process and machine changes that would cut costs for maintenance, electricity, and chemicals.

For example, the privatizers claimed that since they were big corporations, they could buy chemicals in large quantities, and therefore cheaper. Union members countered that Montague could join an existing consortium of small towns that bought chemicals together—and save thousands of dollars.

The workers' plan was challenged, of course, by the privatizers, at another televised hearing. The evidence, however, was overwhelming that union members had developed a cost-saving plan that did not involve wage or job cuts and that kept the facility on a non-profit basis.

In the end, one Selectman's plea that "everyone knows big business runs things better" was greeted with chuckles, mockery, and a vote to keep the plant public.

SOME LESSONS LEARNED

- The fight against privatization must be made public and held in public—people support public facilities that they think are well-run. They don't like overpaid bureaucrats and waste.
- Turn the focus back on management. Talk about eliminating or trimming executive salaries.
- Develop a union proposal on how money can be saved and efficiency improved without cutting jobs or pay. In Montague, workers consulted everyone from the electric company to the federal government and got useful advice.
- Look to the community. Churches and activists can turn out valuable help.
- Emphasize that privatizing a public service means adding a new and unacceptable cost: profit.

MORE ON INVOLVING SUPPORTERS

Chapter 7, "Coalition-Building," provides a wealth of ideas for how unions and worker centers can bring their campaigns into a wider community. Authors in that section explore unions and communities that have fused their work together, finding that "each other's" issues are the same.

Also, don't miss "Taking a Contract Campaign Public" on page 229. It tells how a municipal union prepared members to take a demand beyond the bargaining table and into the public to win health care benefits for the first time.

HOME-BASED WORKERS CREATE A NEW KIND OF STEWARD

by Hetty Rosenstein

The Communications Workers told New Jersey CWA locals in 2005 that the union was beginning an organizing drive for the state's 12,000 home childcare workers. The plan was to get assistance from ACORN community organizers and knock on 12,000 doors.

The childcare workers were registered with the state to care for the children of families receiving subsidized childcare (mostly through Welfare to Work) and were considered to be independent contractors.

Organizing them involved visiting houses, identifying active workers, signing them up, and getting recognition from the state through an executive order. It was a tall order, and CWA locals were asked to lend assistance if they could.

To bring together thousands of contractors working from home, one union turned to a neighborhood approach.

The drive started much as it has in other states, but ended in a victory for a new kind of home care workers union that focuses on building active members. Local 1037 at first had no intention of becoming the childcare local for the state. The local was busy with other organizing, and agreed only to assist in the drive on an ad-hoc basis and to send out its organizers and stewards to knock on doors in a few counties.

Within a few weeks, however, the local built strong relationships with workers and felt that this new kind of organizing needed to be integrated with CWA's worksite philosophy.

CONTRACTORS TO STEWARDS

Local 1037 leaders didn't like the idea of contracting out the campaign or organizing any workers without a real organizing committee. Research into how these units were organized elsewhere led the local to fear that the union was functioning like a customer service agency

and relating to workers through the telephone.

If Local 1037 was going to organize childcare workers, then childcare workers were going to become active and involved members of the union. They were going to define their own issues, and direct the campaign and contract negotiations.

But how do you organize thousands of independent contractors working in their homes throughout the state into a union? The local first turned to a cadre of stewards who attended the local's own Shop Stewards Organizing Institute, two-day overnight trainings that prepare stewards to be involved in new member organizing.

Stewards are the heart and soul of all of the work that Local 1037 does in its units. Stewards engage in contract enforcement, mobilization, organizing, political activity, community services, training, lobbying, and more.

During the training stewards learn how to engage in a member contact, talk about the union at their worksite, and express a vision of organizing that comes from their own experience.

Several Local 1037 stewards worked on the childcare drive and served on the organizing committee with childcare workers themselves. They visited houses and called other childcare workers, helping to collect more than 4,000 cards the union eventually submitted.

WINNING A CONTRACT

In August 2006, then-Governor Jon Corzine signed an executive order recognizing both CWA and the American Federation of State,

County, and Municipal Employees (AFSCME) as the "Child Care Workers Union." Local 1037 now shares a bargaining unit of more than 6,000 home childcare workers with AFSCME Council 1. The first contract was ratified in November 2007.

Now it was time for those leaders to become stewards.

Local 1037 modified its structure. Instead of having worksite shop stewards, organizing committee members became "neighborhood shop stewards," new member-leaders who could represent other childcare workers in their communities. Neighborhood stewards helped get bargaining surveys filled out, car-pooled childcare workers to meetings to elect a bargaining committee, and finally helped to turn out workers to ratify the first contract in November 2007.

Under the new contract, childcare workers are paid through vouchers that parents are given to subsidize their childcare. The union was able to increase the subsidy amounts by 25 percent in less than two years. Parents will now get seniority lists when they select a childcare worker, so they will know who is experienced and who just started. A new grievance procedure now also provides for arbitration of disputes.

FORGING NEW LEADERS

Local 1037 leaders don't entirely know how the new steward system will work out in the end. In some neighborhoods there are dozens of childcare workers and in others there are only a few. But Local 1037 believes that its greatest strength is its structure, which permits the struggle for power to emanate from the workplace, led by a worksite leader.

If the labor movement is going to engage in new forms of organizing, it needs to not lose this critical level of union activism.

Nancy Jimenez, a childcare steward in Newark, said the collective approach to problem-solving transformed her work. "I was a little skeptical at first," she said. "I thought the union was going to be one person coming in to take over. But we are this union."

LOSING DUES CHECK-OFF AND THRIVING

by David Cohen

Kennametal Corp. in western Massachusetts had a long history of bitter fights with United Electrical Workers Local 274.

But when the contract expired in 2010 with no resolution of bargaining, the tool-making company notched up its anti-union attacks. Kennametal announced it would not abide by the dues check-off clause, the arbitration clause, or the union security clause.

In a small shop, collecting dues by hand showed the union's strength.

This was supposed to put pressure on UE Local 274 to accept concessions.

The local decided to collect dues by hand, to show the company that the union wouldn't be intimidated and that members were sticking together. We did not make paying dues the key issue to "keeping the union alive." It was just another thing that had to be done.

Officers thought there was a bigger chance of misplacing checks or losing money if they tried to collect dues weekly. They decided on a monthly collection and posted the total amount owed each month on the in-shop bulletin board. That information was also included on leaflets distributed regularly to keep members updated on negotiations.

Members could either give their dues to a steward or officer, or mail them to the union hall. People paying cash got receipts.

Out of the 75

members, only two refused to pay dues.

It harked back to the days when all dues were collected by hand. If workers got mad about something, they might not pay their dues that month. The stewards or officers would have to spend time with them going over their grievances.

Sometimes the grievances were real and had to be addressed, sometimes the company was lying to a worker about something and blaming it on the union, and other times the worker was just looking for an excuse to not pay up.

Many members paid ahead in their dues, but some were bad at paying bills in general. We had to distinguish why someone was falling behind. Some stewards and officers were better than others at collecting, and at talking to people who were falling behind.

Collecting dues was not the main task of stewards and officers. It was one thing among many: getting members to wear union T-shirts, come to after-work gate meetings, sign petitions, and picket before work. They still had to prepare grievances and Labor Board charges.

The officers who kept the books had to maintain accurate lists of who had paid and how much. They had a complicated job, depositing dozens of checks and lots of cash.

Some members wanted to fight more with backward members than with the company. They wanted monthly lists posted of who was not paying dues. We argued that this would turn the fight internally rather than with the company, and it would give the company targets to work on if people were falling behind.

For six months, until the contract was settled, the union collected dues by hand. New hires had to be talked into signing up. (The company was telling new hires they didn't have to join.) All the new hires joined the union and began paying dues.

Collecting dues by hand showed the strength of the union as an institution in the workplace. Members disagreed on many aspects of the contract struggle, but they were united in keeping the union functioning.

In the end, the local won a contract that protected new hires and fought off the worst concessions.

SURVIVING WITHOUT CHECK-OFF

by Tom Smith

As public workers from Wisconsin to Idaho face legislative efforts to eliminate dues check-off rights, how we fund and sustain our organizations has become a central question.

Here in the right-to-work South, where public employees have never had the right to bargain collectively, we struggle with self-sustainability every day. Here's the good news: while having dues check-off helps, not having it isn't fatal.

I am an organizer and former president of CWA Local 3865 in Tennessee. We organize public higher education workers. In the last decade we have built a non-majority union that's grown from two dozen members on one campus to more than 1,200 in eight cities.

In the 1930s, as modern unionism was taking off, dues check-off did not exist. Unions tried many things. Giving lapel buttons to workers who paid their dues proved very popular for industrial unions, auto workers and electrical workers among them. That method isn't going to cut it these days.

In the early years of our union, elements of our leadership argued that having to hand-collect dues kept the local's leaders and organizer honest.

Rallying for public workers in Tennessee.

This attitude meant attending weekly meetings to make plans to collect dues. Quickly we realized that spending the majority of our time playing bill collector was not part and parcel of union democracy, nor did it help build the kind of political relationships we're aiming for on the job. Stewards need to spend their time listening to co-workers, gathering opinions about how to build the union, organizing meetings, and working to win a fight or save jobs when budget cuts rear their head.

One method we chose for dues collection is the bank draft, where the union deducts dues straight from members' bank accounts. Ideally, this means that when new recruits fill out a membership form they also write down their bank routing number and account number. This is our "dues agreement."

Needless to say, the bank draft adds a new layer of difficulty in signing up members. Not only must the member or staff organizer move the worker into action, but we also have to convince them to give us their damn bank info!

Very few people sign on first contact. A longer relationship must be built. Thus union strategies that are built around a quick campaign "before the boss wakes up" are non-starters for us.

Bank drafts are complicated. We have a number of different drafts depending on pay periods. As anyone who has lived from paycheck to paycheck knows, automatic withdrawals need to be timed so that enough "available funds" are left behind to ensure groceries and gas don't overdraw the account. When possible we deduct dues from the check that does not contain the health insurance premium.

We now know all the local bank routing numbers, so new members signing up can simply put their bank's name. The form specifies savings or checking account, to prevent expensive returns. We ask all new members to sign up for bank draft, instead of giving an option to pay cash, which has increased participation in the automatic deduction.

The amount of work involved with the bank drafts is very large. Staff devote dozens of hours each month to setting them up, adding new members, and dealing with transaction fees, returns that slam the union with an additional fee, and the dreaded "drops" when folks quit.

Thousands of dollars annually are at stake, but it isn't just money. It's politics. Dues are an important expression of our commitment to our union, and one of the greatest resources we have. For us the choice is a simple one: bank draft or stop being a union.

As anti-union lawmakers in other states roll back cherished rights to check-off and bargaining, our sisters and brothers in the North will see the choice before them as clearly as we do down here in the South. We need y'all to keep being union, too.

UNDER RIGHT-TO-WORK LAWS
ORGANIZING UNDER THE GUN

by Paul Ortiz

Florida is not Wisconsin. Wisconsin's history is Robert LaFollette, the Progressive Party, and the birth of public employee unionism.

Conversely, Florida had the Rosewood Massacre and the Ku Klux Klan. A grand jury recently found that "corruption is pervasive at all levels of government."

Republican Governor Rick Scott has signed measures making it harder to vote, moving Florida back toward its Jim Crow past. We are one of several states with no department to enforce wage and hour standards.

Despite these obstacles, faculty members in Florida's public institutions of higher learning have been building unions in our right-to-work state at an outstanding rate. At the University of Florida union density was about 20 percent in 2010. A year later, it's over 40 percent and rapidly rising.

The union positioned itself to use legislative attacks to develop member leadership.

One key impetus was the state legislature's attack on public employee unionism. The Automatic Decertification Bill would have decertified any public employee union with less than half those it represented signed up as members. The cynically named Paycheck Protection Bill would have prohibited unions from deducting dues from paychecks.

While these bills did not pass, they convinced would-be members that public employees are under siege. Equally important to our success was United Faculty of Florida's recent track record of defending the jobs of laid-off employees, both tenured and untenured.

Colleges across the country have made it clear that tenure no longer means a guarantee of job security. We stressed to faculty that the only real guarantee of due process, security of employment, and salary increases is a union contract.

Professors at Florida State University in Tallahassee are organizing just as fast as at University of Florida, as are instructors at our other major research universities. Faculty at Florida's unionized community colleges had already built membership rates of 70 percent and higher.

(In this instance Wisconsin, not coincidentally, was like Florida: six groups of university workers there voted for a union after Governor Scott Walker brought forward his plan to eliminate public employee bargaining.)

EACH MEMBER AN ORGANIZER

In normal times, college instructors tend to work in isolation. We teach our courses, hold office hours, and conduct research mostly as individuals. Our organizing campaign has brought us closer together as colleagues and brother and sister workers. Our campaign adopted the idea that with a bit of peer education, every member can be an organizer.

With the assistance of NEA organizers, we gave members the confidence to conduct office visits, interpret the contract, and speak at departmental meetings about the importance of unionism.

Our best teacher was experience. We met informally several times per week to discuss what recruitment pitches worked and which did not. Our lead organizers coordinated an online volunteer sign-up sheet that ensured member-organizers spread out across the entire bargaining unit.

We discovered that one-on-one conversations with potential members worked best. However, we also garnered new members by speaking to faculty at the end of department meetings. We found out that we needed to modify our informational and recruitment flyers to reflect the divergent experiences of tenure-track and non-tenured instructors and staff.

We held informal social "mixers" where members could update each other on the status of the campaign and just relax and have a good time.

TYING IN POLITICS

Because the state legislature was pushing anti-worker legislation, it was not difficult to weave in the crucial ties between the workplace and politics in our recruitment pitches.

As the rank-and-file coordinator of our organizing drive noted, "We would knock on faculty office doors and start off, 'You know what Scott Walker's doing in Wisconsin? Well, it's coming to Florida, too.' So I guess you could say it was Walker and Scott and the Koch brothers who helped us."

Faculty started to see their union in a different way. It wasn't just about bargaining on campus. It was about the bigger picture of state and national politics, budget cuts to education, and ongoing attacks on public sector workers—us!

For years our union has sponsored rallies and educational events focused on how our students' needs take a back seat to the relentless de-funding of education. Stepping up participation in our central labor council also helped us connect our struggles with those in other sectors of the economy.

Our coordinator observed, "Some new members joined out of solidarity with other public employees. Some started to understand that unions give them a voice in government for all kinds of issues they care about—not just pay and benefits, but the future of education and our state as a whole."

INVOLVING NEW MEMBERS

Our members devoted themselves to urging representatives in Tallahassee to vote for public education and against the anti-union bills.

This is also how we encouraged our newest members to get involved immediately in union activities. Many newer members found it easier to call a state senator than to make an office visit. We emphasized that both activities were critical to our union's survival.

While professors are vilified as snobby elitists on cable news, we discovered that many faculty share a profound sense of alienation about their labor.

Our organizing campaign has given faculty the space to think about how valuable our labor power is to the world. One new member in the humanities said, "I joined UFF because we produce the most important products in our society: original ideas, new ways of thinking, and perhaps most importantly, criticisms of our past and present reality that may be unpopular but necessary."

Most faculty members still don't see themselves as labor activists. But building a successful union movement allowed them increasingly to think of the relationship between their work and the crises in the larger society that affect higher education and democracy.

STEWARDS COMMITTEE JUMP-STARTS ACTION ACROSS UNIONS

by Bill Franks, Ron Blascoe, and Barbara Smith

Even before the uprising that saw a hundred thousand take to the streets to oppose Governor Scott Walker's attacks on public services and public workers, stewards in Wisconsin state employee unions knew how to work together across unions to stir up action.

A seemingly minor issue sparked a mass grievance by workers at the Wisconsin Department of Workforce Development back in the '90s, in one state building in downtown Madison.

When management issued an edict banning all smoking on the premises, stewards from one union called a meeting of stewards for all locals in the building, which included professional, administrative, and technical employees.

Working together, stewards in sister unions can shake off mistrust and lead campaigns.

The workers thought smokers should have some place to go. Together we hatched a strategy: "We Demand a Veranda."

We filed a group grievance co-signed by 200 employees. Stewards knew that managers would probably just stonewall through arbitration unless they felt some pressure to settle.

Our union's staff organizer helped us set up an email group and we started sending blow-by-blow accounts of the grievance process to hundreds in the building. Two joint leaflets—explaining the reasonableness of our proposals and the unreasonableness of management's response—went to all 800 mailboxes in the building.

When management's reply came back, "Grievance denied. No contract violation," everyone knew about it. Finally, after growing embarrassment, management relented and reversed the policy.

The issue was resolved in months, but the cross-union stewards committee that formed out of that fight proved to have lasting value.

EVERY TUESDAY

Stewards know that a majority of grievances will not result in relief being granted. The lesson from that mass grievance was that we make our own power when we involve co-workers in concerted action.

Stewards have been meeting Tuesdays at lunchtime since that beginning. One Tuesday a month all union members in the building are invited.

After Governor Walker was elected in 2010 but before he took office, the committee put out two newsletters warning fellow workers and providing facts on the real situation of state employees and the state budget. When Walker released his plans to bust our unions in February 2011, we immediately set up a building meeting.

Later, when Walker, with a straight face, decreed a State Employee Recognition Day, we proclaimed our own State Employee Depreciation Day, with a ceremony on the Capitol steps in which Wisconsin corporations received spoof awards.

In an earlier project, members signed a petition to support the building's janitors in their union drive. Hundreds signed, even the head of the agency. When stewards peacefully delivered the petition on their lunch hour, it earned them a police interview in their cubicles the next day. Stewards stood strong and kept their cool.

Communication is key. An early project was the campaign to get a bulletin board. Management designated an obscure spot and overruled the union's choice for a prominent location, citing danger from push pins scattering on the floor.

Noting there were other bulletin boards in the hallways, stewards posted throughout the building yellow triangular caution signs labeled "Falling Pins Zone." After the laughter died down, we got our prime spot.

UNION ORIENTATION

A few years ago, big snowstorms led to slips and broken bones all over town. In our building icy steps went unshoveled after snow removal was privatized. Management's answer was to send out a safety memo advising employees to "walk like a duck" to keep from slipping.

Stewards immediately filed a grievance and put out a pamphlet to members explaining how to file an incident report about any accident at work. This was important to gather statistics about slips and falls, and also could be useful to get work absences covered by worker's comp.

The grievance was denied, but the relief sought was granted. Management sent out maintenance staff to shovel the steps.

In another project, we organized a union orientation for kids on "Take Your Kids to Work Day." Management said OK before realizing what we were up to. We showed a slide show about child labor and did a participatory play called "Trouble in the Henhouse" about organizing chickens.

The actors wore homemade chicken costumes; the kids joined in with chicken masks and clucked in the right places. Candy "feed" was consumed, and humans and chickens alike sang "Solidarity Forever" at the end.

COMMON INTERESTS

Working across union barriers has been less difficult in practice than expected, as front-line stewards found their common interests stronger than their differences. The two large statewide locals had more materials to contribute; the other two locals had less than 100 members each but were more nimble.

Spending time together has helped build up trust, though sometimes stewards from the smaller unions have to warn the big locals not to dominate with their internal issues.

But the stewards committee has received a chilly reception from elected union leaders, who are suspicious of this independent body. All our work is done without paid staff time or formal backing.

Leaders have cut off photocopying privileges and locked up one local's button-making machine after its use in an effective campaign. But stewards have voted with their feet by remaining active with the committee in spite of most leaders' disapproval.

Over time, stewards from other buildings downtown have begun to join the meetings. Stewards come to get suggestions and courage. The committee has proven useful as a stewards training ground, on FMLA or whistleblower language, for instance. This training function has become more valuable as senior stewards are retiring at record rates.

Most important, we work to keep things light even when there are differences. Good-humored swearing is an institution, and laughter is often heard echoing from our meeting room.

Our local's bureaucracy is often crippled by indecision, fear of member involvement, and lack of practice in activism. In this context, a small group of people can be surprisingly effective at jump-starting motion that captures the imagination of members and gets results.

Chapter Six

DEFENDING EVERYONE

Tens of thousands of protesters marched in Atlanta in July 2011 to protest an anti-immigrant state law.

LET'S TALK IMMIGRATION IN THE UNION

by Tiffany Ten Eyck

When New York's governor announced in 2007 that the state would stop asking people who wanted driver's licenses for proof of citizenship, a firestorm of anger erupted—so hot that the governor rescinded his proposal.

Guillermo Perez, a labor educator and the president of the Albany, New York, chapter of the Labor Council for Latin American Advancement (LCLAA), was appalled.

Support on paper doesn't translate into support in the ranks without an education program.

"Seventy percent of the people were opposed? How is that possible?" he asked other immigrant rights activists. "I couldn't believe that there was this much hatred in New York. So many people in New York City are immigrants."

In Perez's view, the anti-immigrant backlash illustrated just how unions, community organizations, and faith groups were failing to educate people.

TALKING IMMIGRATION

"The official position of the state AFL-CIO, the national AFL-CIO, and the Catholic Church is welcoming to immigrants," he said. "The AFL-CIO unanimously passed a resolution in 2000 in support of amnesty for the undocumented, but it didn't come with an education program for members.

"We have these powerful organizations backing us, but the grassroots—the rank and file of unions, members of parishes—just weren't there, on why the immigrants are here and who they are."

So a small group of local activists began discussing an education program. The result was "Let's Talk Immigration," a project of the ARISE Civil Rights of Immigrants Task Force, the local chapter of

LCLAA, and the Labor-Religion Coalition of the Capital District, in affiliation with the "Truth About Immigrants" campaign of the New York Immigration Coalition.

They gathered resources from labor educators and from Interfaith Worker Justice, a national coalition of faith-based pro-worker groups. The idea was to create an interactive workshop—nothing academic or dry, and definitely no PowerPoint.

The hope was that "maybe we wouldn't convert people," Perez said, "but we would give them something to think about, to be more open in the future. Where else are they going to hear the stories of immigrants? Why are they here? What happened to them?"

FACTS WITH PERSPECTIVE

The workshop team wanted to provide facts, yes, but also exercises that would help participants see their own immigration histories. They wanted some perspective on the history of immigrants in the United States, and discussion on how to bring the debate back to their unions or churches. The goal was a curriculum that a central labor council or a union could use.

"A lot of materials were four or six hours," Perez recalls. "Our goal was 90 minutes."

The curriculum they created includes:

Introductions, in which people tell when their families came to this country, and from where. Participants can tell their families' stories and whether their own immigrant heritage has been a source of pain or pride.

A historical quotes matching game. On one side of the page are ugly quotes from four influential U.S. leaders, condemning various immigrant groups. On the other side are listed previously stigmatized groups (Italians, Irish, Greeks, Poles) and representatives of the current wave of immigrants, such as Mexicans and Caribbeans.

The lesson is that anti-immigrant backlash is nothing new, that politicians have always condemned immigrants—including some of the participants' own grandparents—as criminals, barbarians, scoundrels, riffraff, and terrorists.

A true-false section, with statements about undocumented immigrants' participation in the workforce (higher than non-immigrants');

the contributions undocumented workers make to Social Security and to taxes (billions annually); connections to crime and terrorism (none); and the impact of immigrant labor on depressing wages (slight for the worst-educated).

For example, "The IRS recently determined that between 1996 and 2003 undocumented workers paid $50 billion in federal taxes." It's true. Detailed sources are included.

Role plays to get people talking. One takes place at a union membership meeting that discusses whether the union should support the organizing of immigrant workers in the area, including the undocumented.

Another scenario has a resolution offered to support a local workers center with $5,000 a year and participation on its board. Some members are opposed, some support the idea, and some start out undecided.

In another role play, a church leader with a growing Latino congregation wants the group to openly advocate on behalf of undocumented immigrants. Another leader says the church should not get involved in controversial political matters.

"In my experience, engaging union people and people of faith on this topic is not that difficult," Perez said. "I'm convinced that once people have good information and really think about the issue, they'll become much more supportive of immigrant workers and their families."

IMMIGRANT DEFENSE ACTION NETWORKS

by Jerry Mead-Lucero

When the Department of Homeland Security announced a policy that gave employers a freer hand to punish workers with mismatched Social Security numbers, a committee of unions, workers' centers, and immigrant rights groups in Chicago swung into action.

The Chicago Committee Against No Match has organized hundreds of activists throughout the area to respond immediately to the firing and harassment of workers whose names come up on no-match letters.

The Social Security Administration has issued about 100,000 of these no-match letters to employers in recent years, despite a finding from the agency's inspector general that 12.7 million of the 17.8 million discrepancies in SSA's database belonged to native-born workers.

The efforts of the union to defend immigrant workers says much more to them what a union is all about than any organizing flyer.

Led by the United Electrical Workers (UE) and the Chicago Workers' Collaborative (CWC) workers center, advocates in Chicago aren't waiting for lawsuits and legal wrangling to defend workers, however.

Their goal is to put workers' needs at the center of the immigration debate and raise the employer's cost for abusing no-match letters, said Mark Meinster, a UE representative in Chicago.

"Since we launched the rapid-response network, we have saved 351 workers their jobs," said Tim Bell, CWC's executive director. "Those are 351 workers who would have probably gone from living-wage jobs to making less than minimum wage. This is a winning strategy that groups have to spread around the country."

URGENT ACTION NETWORK

The network's first move was to set up a hotline for workers to use when employers targeted them because of no-match letters. The network fielded hundreds of calls in its first three months and stepped into 11 workplace disputes.

There are several responses deployed depending on the type of call, Meinster said. Legal residents are routed to the team of attorneys, which contacts the employer. The attorneys educate confused employers, explaining that no-match letters—because they're not a reliable indication of legal status by themselves—should not be used as grounds for discipline or dismissal.

News about the hotline spread as the network distributed flyers at community events, worked English- and Spanish-language media, and convinced elected officials to refer cases to them. The network's backbone comes from a dozen workshops, mostly held within a 50-mile radius around Chicago, Bell said.

Drawing together religious leaders, immigrant rights activists, community group staffers, union members, attorneys, local politicians, and concerned residents, the trainings prepare activists to understand and quickly respond to no-match situations in their area. The goal for a full regional mobilization is to bring out 300-500 people on short notice for an action, Bell said.

ESCALATING ACTION

When workers already fired because of a no-match letter call the hotline, the legal team looks for health and safety violations at their workplace, and reminds the employer that it could face a discrimination or labor-law violation lawsuit if it singled out particular workers.

If a no-match situation places a large group of employees at risk, organizers quickly reach into the community surrounding the workplace. Organizers call a meeting and instruct workers about their rights. They distribute bilingual materials explaining legalities, such as the rule that prohibits employers from checking documents after three days from hiring. The workers map out an action plan with the network's activists, delivering petitions to the owner and inviting religious leaders and media to visit plant managers. The organizers also help workers educate their co-workers—including those who are native-born—so they can prepare a coordinated response.

The network reaches for confrontational tactics, like community rallies outside the plant, when an employer is unresponsive. In extreme cases, when all employees could be fired, organizers assist workers to prepare a strike and mobilize the full network.

REAL-WORLD TESTS

The network moved quickly from theory to action. At Peacock Engineering, a food-container company with four plants in Chicago's northwest suburbs, management attempted to use no-match letters to shed a majority of its permanent workforce—comprising several hundred employees—and replace them with temporary workers.

Pressure by the network's legal team and internal organizing by the workers, which built up to a threatened walk-out, convinced management to fold.

The network also has uncovered cases where union locals unaware of the letters' flaws have left their members undefended. Emanuel Castro, an employee of Utility Builders in Morris, Illinois, and a member of Laborers Local 25, turned to his union when he and fellow workers were threatened with dismissal because of no-match letters.

When union officials told him they were powerless, he contacted the hotline. Although Utility Builders workers were fired, Local 25 filed grievances after the network worked with the union to persuade leaders to fight cases of no-match among their members.

ORGANIZING INROADS

Creating the no-match network has required significant investments of time, money, and resources without the immediate promise of adding dues-paying members to union rolls. But for UE, the effort is seen as a down payment.

"We view this as a big-time organizing opportunity, because we think workers are going to be in motion on this issue [and] looking for assistance on fighting back," Meinster said.

Their strategy looks to be paying off. No-match battles identify key worker leaders, who can move co-workers to sign union cards. Workers facing the threat of no-match firings at Food 4 Less, a grocery store chain, have injected new life into a campaign by Food and Commercial Workers Local 881.

"The workers who are now helping UFCW organize at Food 4 Less are the same workers who in months past were the least likely to contact the union," said Moises Zavala, a Local 881 organizer. "The no-match situation and the efforts of the union to fight no-match letters says much more to immigrant workers what a union is all about than any union brochure or flyer."

No-match letters may become the new plant-closing bogeyman—a tool to strike fear into workers who question low pay and poor working conditions. For forward-looking unions, joining with community groups to fight no-match letters can show immigrant workers anxious to challenge their employer that they have a home in labor.

PROTECTING LESBIAN, GAY, AND TRANSGENDER MEMBERS

by Donna Cartwright

The union can use the contract to defend vulnerable minorities, even in hostile jurisdictions.

Too many lesbian, gay, bisexual, or transgender workers are simply fired if they come out—or are "outed" involuntarily—at work. LGBT workers may be fired outright, or they may be harassed until they quit.

In many states, they have no recourse under the law. Their unions are the only place they can turn to if they run into bias on the job, from discrimination to denial of benefits. Unions can prevent such treatment by negotiating for expanded nondiscrimination language.

Many contracts already bar unfair treatment based on race, sex, religion, national origin, and other categories. These clauses should be expanded to include "sexual orientation," which would protect gay, lesbian, and bisexual workers, and "gender identity and expression," which would protect transgender workers.

BUCK UP EXISTING LANGUAGE

If gay, lesbian, and bisexual workers are already covered by your contract language, but not transgender workers, try to add gender identity/expression protections. This may help more people than it might seem at first, because sometimes gay, lesbian, bisexual, and even straight workers, as well as transgender employees, are discriminated against based on gender stereotypes (men who are perceived as effeminate, or women who are perceived as masculine).

Here is the nondiscrimination language from Newspaper Guild/CWA's contract with the Boston Globe:

> *The employer agrees that it will not discriminate ... by reason of race, creed, color, national origin, political or religious views, union position, sex, sexual orientation, gender identity or expression, age, physical or*

mental disability, marital status, physical appearance apart from dress beyond bona fide occupational requirements, parenthood or child-bearing capacity.

Corporate human resources policies often include such protections, but unlike contract language, corporate policies usually lack an impartial enforcement procedure. If your contract is not open for re-negotiation, the union and the employer can exchange side letters of agreement stating that nondiscrimination protections will apply to LGBT workers.

When negotiating for nondiscrimination language, it's important to remember that there is no real cost attached to such protection. If the employer wants the union to give something in return, tell him that this is a non-economic issue as well as a question of fundamental fairness. Even if you can't negotiate nondiscrimination language immediately, there are other avenues to pursue.

First, check applicable state and local laws to see if they contain LGBT nondiscrimination language. Twenty states and more than 100 municipalities have legislation prohibiting discrimination based on sexual orientation, while 12 states and more than 80 municipalities have laws covering gender identity or expression.

Existing contract language may also be helpful. Almost all contracts prohibit discharge or discipline without just and sufficient cause (or similar language), and an arbitrator or grievance panel may rule that simply being LGBT is not sufficient cause for being fired, suspended, transferred, or demoted.

EXPANDING BENEFITS

Hundreds of major private sector companies, and many public employers, now have domestic partner benefits, which allow LGBT workers to provide health insurance, and sometimes other benefits, to their partners. You can raise the issue when benefits plans are revised at the beginning of each year, as well as at contract expiration.

If your state has constitutional or statutory language prohibiting such benefits for public employees, alternative language can be developed that allows workers to designate an unrelated adult beneficiary for health and other benefits.

Many insurance policies prohibit coverage of any transgender-related condition or treatment, from surgery to hormone therapy and other procedures. If your benefits plan has such restrictions, try to get them removed.

An increasing number of major employers do cover transgender health care or are considering doing so. They include, for example, the city and county of San Francisco and the University of Michigan in the public sector, and Chrysler, Pacific Gas & Electric, and Keyspan Energy in the private sector.

COVER EVERYONE

More strategies include:

- Make sure that pension and life insurance plans allow LGBT workers to designate their partners as beneficiaries.
- Ensure that bereavement leave is interpreted to cover civil unions and domestic partners.
- Encourage employers to train their human resources staffs in LGBT issues, and have plans in place if workers come out on the job. Advance planning beats improvising in a crisis atmosphere.
- Ensure that partners are welcome at company (and union) picnics and holiday parties.
- Arrange for transgender workers to be issued gender-appropriate identification badges, and allow them to make necessary changes to their employment records; provide access to bathrooms based on workers' self-identification; and provide for reasonable accommodation in locker and shower rooms.

DEMONSTRATE SUPPORT

If you need to demonstrate that there is strong support in your union for LGBT members' issues, a petition can help. Try to get well-respected people who are known as fair-minded to sign first, and then get a representative group of fellow workers to add their names.

Both management and union officials may be more likely to agree to protect a vulnerable minority if they see that there is widespread support for fairness.

[Pride at Work provides a five-hour training program on bargaining for LGBT issues. Find out more at prideatwork.org.]

MAKING SURE ALL FAMILIES BENEFIT

by Julie Robert and Helen Ho

When Michigan voters went to the polls in November 2004, they were asked to consider Proposal 2, which asked whether "the union of one man and one woman in marriage shall be the only agreement recognized as a marriage or similar union for any purpose."

To most voters, Proposal 2 was about restricting the legal definition of marriage to a union between a man and a woman. Many underestimated the importance of the proposal's seemingly benign phrase, "for any purpose."

Health benefits don't have to be based on legal status or sexual orientation.

Proposal 2 passed, and although supporters of the amendment insisted that it would not affect domestic partner benefits (which allow lesbian, gay, and transgender couples to receive health coverage through their partner's benefit plans), the right to these benefits was quickly challenged in court.

LEGAL LIMBO

While lower courts upheld the provision of benefits, the Michigan Court of Appeals issued an opinion in February 2007 that prevented public employers from providing benefits to anybody except the legal spouse of the employee and their dependent children.

Courts in the state of Michigan interpreted Proposal 2 broadly. Same-sex couples in Michigan who received benefits under the terms of "domestic partnership" were in a state of legal limbo.

For those working under a collective bargaining agreement, all benefits were expected to remain in place until the agreements expired. When these contracts expired, however, it would be illegal for employers to offer benefits under the rubric of domestic partnerships of any kind.

Union members and other university employees receiving same-sex domestic partner benefits were threatened with no longer receiving health care—or even alternative health care options like COBRA.

BENEFITS FOR ALL

The union representing graduate student employees at the University of Michigan, the Graduate Employees Organization (GEO), launched a "Benefits for All" campaign to respond to the post-Proposal 2 political climate. The campaign pushed for a "designated beneficiaries" plan that would protect workers' rights to health care while accommodating the law.

A designated beneficiaries plan enables employees to extend coverage to another adult and that adult's dependent children. Instead of basing eligibility on marital status, a designated beneficiaries plan would be based on criteria including shared property, joint living (such as joint bank accounts), and shared responsibility for minors.

Like existing benefits structures, the plan includes provisions to safeguard it against misuse. This type of plan, while new to the University of Michigan, has been used successfully by other organizations and provides benefits for all while accommodating Michigan law.

For GEO members, this would mean shared benefits would be provided based on shared living arrangements, rather than being based on legal status or sexual orientation. "Having a family is a personal decision that these kinds of politics shouldn't interfere with," said GEO member Sue Sierra.

SUPPORTING EQUAL RIGHTS

GEO was one of the groups that successfully lobbied the University of Michigan to change its bylaws in 1993 to ban discrimination of any kind—including based on sexual orientation. This bylaw allowed for the implementation of same-sex domestic partner benefits in 1994.

In 2005, GEO negotiated anti-discrimination language around gender identity and gender expression into its contract and got the university as a whole to do the same. The GEO contract also guaranteed benefits for transgendered individuals and their partners, regardless of the legal sex of either person.

GEO also advocated for, and later passed, a resolution at the Teachers union (AFT) national convention that calls on its local unions to bargain for transgender-inclusive health care benefits.

For GEO's "Benefits for All" campaign, members of the union's solidarity and political action committee are forming coalitions with other unions on campus and across the state, with faculty and staff at the university, and with community and campus groups.

Kiara Vigil, a member of the political action committee, says it is determined to "raise the level of public discourse" surrounding domestic partner benefits because it's "an important social justice issue."

CONSTITUENCY CAUCUSES CAN SPEAK TO MANY NEEDS

by Guillermo Perez

When New York state made national news in 2007 with a flap about driver's licenses for undocumented immigrants, the state AFL-CIO supported the immigrants but wasn't out in front. Neither was another supporter, the Catholic Church.

But as chair of the Albany/Capital District chapter of the Labor Council for Latin American Advancement (LCLAA), I was getting media calls every other day. We were it.

Together with Jobs with Justice and a local sanctuary group, our LCLAA chapter held two press conferences and a rally in front of the Rensselaer County office building, home to County Clerk Frank Merola. Merola and other local politicians were on national TV bashing immigrants. We were there to say, "Stop stereotyping the undocumented as criminals and terrorists. Issuing driver's licenses will make the roads safer and bring people out of the shadows."

And we did all this as an affiliate of the AFL-CIO and Change to Win federations. LCLAA gave us the chance to do grassroots activism within the official structures.

FIVE CAUCUSES

LCLAA is one of five "constituency groups" recognized by the AFL-CIO and CTW that serve as independent ethnic, racial, gender, or sexual orientation-based caucuses within the two federations. Arguably four of them owe their existence to the first one, the Coalition of Black Trade Unionists.

CBTU was founded by African-American labor leaders who disagreed with the decision of the AFL-CIO executive board, under then-president George Meany, to remain neutral in the 1972 Nixon/McGovern election.

Identity-based groups can push their unions to be a broader force for social justice.

CBTU declared itself to be a "progressive forum for black workers to bring their special issues within unions as well as act as a bridge between organized labor and the black community."

Other caucuses emerged soon after: LCLAA in 1973, the Coalition of Labor Union Women in 1974, the Asian Pacific American Labor Alliance in 1992, and the LGBT-identified group, Pride At Work, in 1999.

Trying to accurately gauge the size and influence of these groups is difficult. As with many grassroots organizations, accepting their own promotional statements regarding their numbers and level of activism is problematic.

At least some local chapters exist only on paper and in cyberspace. And even where the chapters have active members, the activism of many seems to consist only of the occasional fundraising banquet and a small scholarship fund for kids. They seem more like the Kiwanis than like union activists dedicated to advancing the cause of their constituents. But even these chapters have helped to recruit rank-and-file members of color to become more involved in their unions.

LOCAL AND STATEWIDE

Our LCLAA chapter began seven years ago when staff and rank and filers from several public sector unions came together. While we can't boast of any well-attended banquets, we can point to local and statewide initiatives that have benefited from our participation:

We're involved in a project to **integrate our area construction trades,** and we're part of a community coalition that aims to negotiate "community benefit agreements" for development projects in order to assure a more equitable distribution of the jobs generated by such projects.

We organized a **statewide summit of educators and community**

activists to address the achievement gap of Latino children in New York state, and we testified before a local school board to support funding for dual language programs.

We organized several **rallies for immigration reform.**

We produced 800 wallet-size **Miranda rights cards** in English and Spanish that were distributed to immigrants through a local sanctuary group of which we are a founding member.

Working with other groups, we developed a **curriculum to teach rank and filers the facts about immigrants**.

We hosted an event as part of Hispanic Heritage Month that raised money to **bring Mexican unionists to the 2008 Labor Notes conference**.

CROSS-UNION STRENGTH

Constituency groups have the potential to strengthen the labor movement, beyond focusing on the constituency's particular issues. Because each chapter must draw from a required number of unions, they create cross-union coalitions around common interests and develop new activist-leaders, many of whom become more active in their own unions as a result of becoming active in their constituency group chapter.

And they can bring visibility to fights for social justice both inside the labor movement and outside it, among civic, community, and faith-based organizations. In this way people see the labor movement not as a special interest but as a force for social and economic justice.

Visit a constituency group's national website to get a listing of local chapters. If there is no chapter in the area, consider forming one. Charter requirements vary: you will need at least 10 to 25 members from three to five different unions.

If there's any pitfall to watch out for it is becoming overly dependent on any one union for your funding or support. Chapters need to be passionately independent, or they stand to lose credibility among their constituents, and with it, their ability to move unions in a more progressive and inclusive direction.

WINNING SICK LEAVE AT THE CITYWIDE LEVEL

by Young Workers United

Young Workers United, a multi-racial San Francisco organization of young and immigrant workers, won an historic victory when they achieved citywide paid sick day legislation in November 2007.

Voters approved a local measure by 61 percent, making San Francisco the first place in the nation where workers were guaranteed the right to a paid sick day for themselves and their families.

The paid sick days ordinance represents another step towards raising standards in the low-wage, non-union service sector in San Francisco.

A grassroots coalition defused business opposition by taking the campaign into many different communities.

Young Workers United works with young people in restaurants and on campuses to improve their working conditions. "There have been times when I've been sick and dragged myself to work anyway," said Matt Garron, a YWU member and bartender. "It was a choice between my health and my rent. Nobody should have to make that choice."

According to the Institute for Women's Policy Research, just 51 percent of all workers in the U.S. have paid sick days, and only one in three have paid days to care for children who are ill.

BUILDING A COALITION

Young Workers United members made paid sick days a priority for 2006 and formed a coalition of community groups, unions, and other organizations that represent low-income parents, workers, immigrants, and youth.

The Coalition for Paid Sick Days, led by YWU, is composed of the Chinese Progressive Association, Committee of Interns and Residents (CIR), St. Peters Housing Committee, Rise Up! Grocery Workers, Parent Voices, and UNITE HERE Local 2.

YWU chose those groups because they represent many of the people who lack paid sick days. The coalition wanted to make sure the law covered everybody working in San Francisco, with no minimum hour requirement.

When opponents complained that the law covered even part-time, temporary, and domestic workers, the coalition pointed to its slogan: "Everyone Deserves Paid Sick Days."

The initiative had a tiered structure to protect small businesses. Under the law, workers at businesses that employ fewer than 10 people, including those employed through franchises or chains, can accrue up to 40 hours, or five sick days.

All others accrue up to 72 hours, or nine days. Workers can use the hours to care for themselves, children, parents, or other relatives.

Also, unmarried workers can designate one other person that they may care for. The coalition wanted to guarantee that those with changing and diverse families are treated with the same respect and have the same rights as traditional, nuclear families and those with the legal right to marry.

GOING STRAIGHT TO VOTERS

The coalition made a strategic decision to place the measure on the ballot rather than lobbying the city's Board of Supervisors to adopt the law.

YWU knew it would face fierce resistance from the business community, which would use all of its political influence and money to fight the law at the board. Their power came from the people of San Francisco, who overwhelmingly supported paid sick days in polls.

"This was definitely a grassroots campaign," said Dante Grant of YWU. "We sat together in a room covered with butcher paper, mapping out districts, creating a media plan, training ourselves to gain endorsements and speak on the issue."

The campaign strategy focused on educating and mobilizing our constituencies—workers, parents, immigrants, and union members—to get the message out. The coalition ran a $15,000 campaign, spending the majority of the funds on producing 100,000 pieces of literature.

The tri-lingual English, Cantonese, and Spanish literature featured members of the coalitions' organizations, including a taqueria worker, a hairdresser, a grocery worker, and parents.

Each group focused on outreach strategies that fit their constituencies, as well as participating in joint events. RISE Up! reached out to grocery worker activists to get the message across to other union members and YWU concentrated on outreach to community college students.

The Chinese Progressive Association and St. Peter's focused on Chinatown and the Mission District. CIR worked through residents at San Francisco's public general hospital to mobilize health care professionals.

STAYING POSITIVE

The coalition made sure to have a positive, pro-worker message. "We didn't want to demonize workers and appeal to consumer fears about illness," said YWU member Naomi Nakamura. "Instead, we wanted to show how sick days are a human right and necessary in a caring, compassionate community."

Since the passage of the bill, the coalition has continued community outreach in order to enforce the new law.

Chapter Seven

COALITION-BUILDING

A reform administration in the United Teachers Los Angeles promoted civil disobedience to protest layoffs, working alongside community and parent groups.

WHAT A LASTING UNION-COMMUNITY ALLIANCE LOOKS LIKE

by Jeff Crosby

Workers and homeowners, union members and community activists—all had a reason to march against Bank of America in spring 2009. In Lynn, Massachusetts, our protest was another step in building the relationship between unionized working people and working-class community organizations, especially among immigrants. It's a relationship that the North Shore Labor Council has been carefully nurturing for years.

The march brought together 300 union members and community allies, both to support "labor's issue"—the Employee Free Choice Act (EFCA), which Bank of America had attacked—and to denounce the bank's home foreclosures. Jobs with Justice had led 30 protests of Bank of America across the state, and our alliance in Lynn produced the largest and most diverse.

Union members and community members marched for 'each other's' issues—and found out they were the same.

People joined from the street in a mile-long march through a foreclosure-hit neighborhood adjacent to the downtown bank. Two community members gave unplanned testimony about the seizure of their homes by predatory lenders.

A city councilor who belongs to my union (IUE-CWA Local 201, the largest in the council) spoke about the impact of foreclosures on his neighborhood. A worker who had organized the local waste water treatment plant spoke of management's campaign of intimidation and firings.

The goal, in the words of council organizer Rosa Blumenfeld, was to reframe EFCA as a fight for the community and working people in general, not as a payback to a "special interest"—us, the unions. Boston television and the local Spanish-language papers covered the protest.

Lynn, an old mill town of 95,000 people 16 miles north of Boston, is the site of the longest continuous large-scale manufacturing in the United States. The shoe industry began here in the 1830s, overlapping in the 20th century with General Electric's production of aircraft engines. GE still makes them here in a plant with about 2,000 members of Local 201. The town is changing as it becomes home to Dominicans and Guatemalans, but also Russians, Africans, and Cambodians.

The rally was preceded by weeks of coalition meetings, where the common program of protest against foreclosures and for EFCA was worked out together. The lines separating us are not sharp: union members are losing homes and community members can see the benefit of organizing unions.

SENDING DOWN ROOTS

The roots of the alliance go back much further. Years ago the North Shore Labor Council made a strategic decision to build an alliance with community and faith-based groups. The council wanted to tie together largely white union members and the fast-growing pro-union (but often non-union) immigrant communities. We took on practical work:

- A dozen years ago unions started a program to train new machinists, working with the Essex County Community Organization, a church- and temple-based coalition. While other job-training programs were shutting down, ours trained and placed some 180 machinists.

- Electoral and legislative work with a largely Latino voter empowerment group—housed at the Local 201 hall—led to strategy discussions on the electoral front. When the local Democratic Party didn't support the Obama campaign early on, Local 201 opened its phone lines to Lynn for Obama activists, and the close relationship has continued as the Obama group morphed into Lynn for Change after the campaign.

- Two years ago the school employees union, AFSCME Local 1736, lent critical leadership and an extraordinary membership mobilization to the election of Maria Carrasco to the school board. White union members campaigned with her in white neighborhoods to give her easier access to their neighbors. Carrasco is the only person of color to hold an elected position in Lynn, which is only about half white. She has become a staunch voice for both the unions and Lynn's communities of color, recently attending an AFL-CIO Central Labor Council training conference and chairing the Bank of America rally.

EDUCATION AND POLITICS

The labor council rejects the "lowest common denominator" approach, preferring to address tough issues, educate, and build an increasingly higher level of political unity.

The council sponsors films and speakers, including a visit by progressive Senator Jorge Robledo from Colombia. Fifteen union and community leaders held a successful study group over a summer on corporate globalization (or neoliberalism). Bilingual readings and a popular education approach were used.

Union workers whose forefathers immigrated from Ireland and Italy described the Lynn that their parents or great-grandparents found upon arrival. Then immigrants from the Dominican Republic described what Lynn was like when they got there in recent decades. The discussion drew a sharp contrast between pre- and post-1980s Lynn. The negative impact of privatization, deregulation, free trade, and union-bashing on the lives of working people here was very clear.

The purpose was both to educate participants on what we are up against and to weld a closer unity among the leaders of the different working-class organizations, to better withstand inevitable stress between us in the future.

Such stresses are addressed. Immigrants who are union members, unaccustomed to legalistic grievance procedures to handle work problems, grow frustrated. Trusted union allies try to help get issues resolved.

In the run-up to the Bank of America protest, it became clear that some older union members bought into the right-wing populist argument that poor workers—especially Blacks and Latinos—brought on the economic crisis by taking home loans they couldn't afford. Their bumper stickers ("honk if I am paying your mortgage") dot Lynn.

We take responsibility to challenge these ideas. We explain to members that financial firms packaging and reselling home loans changed the mortgage industry. We put on an education program by Labor Notes on the causes of the financial crisis: lax financial regulation, stagnant wages, huge corporate debt. Member Tom O'Shea wrote articles in the Local 201 *News,* like "Why I Should Care about Someone Else's Mortgage." Nothing was swept under the rug. The resistance died down.

In a small council with limited resources, doing one thing means not doing something else. Less attention has been paid to municipal elections in other towns, and the council's activist base among more conservative local unions is not what it should be. We don't accept these weaknesses as permanent.

In the short term, the right choices resulted in a successful protest. In the long term, we intend to redefine what the labor movement is all about.

PUBLIC EMPLOYEES FIGHT TO SAVE SERVICES AND JOBS

by Carol Lambiase

Public employees in Norwich, Connecticut, a former mill town of about 37,000, are organizing to preserve jobs and services and to get their scheduled wage increases. Our campaign includes departmental meetings, marshaling the facts about what members do, finding allies, meeting with legislators, and finding better ways to run the city.

Members worked hard to let residents know what they were getting for their tax dollars.

Norwich was hit hard by the recession and declining grants from the state government. The city depends on this money. The Youth and Family Services agency, for example, receives nearly $700,000 a year, but only $76,000 comes directly from the city.

In March 2010 members of United Electrical Workers Local 222 in the City Hall Employees Union—who work in records, recreation, planning, human services, public works, community development, finance, the senior center, and the fire department—turned out in force at the city council budget meeting and had their worst fears realized.

The City Manager proposed to meet a budget shortfall by eliminating positions and reducing hours. Union leaders proposed a more equitable solution that would not jeopardize vital services, but in the end members voted to put off scheduled wage increases for a year in order to restore all the positions.

This was the second year in a row members took a wage freeze and sacrificed unequally. Union leaders vowed to prevent it from happening again.

BLUEPRINT FOR SAVING SERVICES

Beginning in September 2010, a strategic planning committee began meeting, open to all members. It developed a blueprint:

- Public education about the value and role of city services
- Building community support
- Engaging the City Manager and other political figures early on
- Scrutiny of city finances
- Developing alternative solutions to the budget shortfall.

The first step was lunchtime meetings with members in all nine departments. A two-person team developed questions and distributed them in advance. The idea was to compile the services members provide in a way that could be used publicly, whether with city council members, for an op-ed, or for a brochure.

Members were asked to look at their jobs in terms of essential services. What would the impact to the community be if these services were reduced or terminated?

What would be the best personal interest stories or examples to use? What residents or agencies or community allies benefited from the services and should be brought into the campaign? What alternatives to layoffs should be proposed?

It was an A-ha! experience for many members. A picture was snapped of each department's workers—the proverbial "human face."

The results were compiled and distributed among members. They reveal a striking relationship between city services, quality of life, and public safety.

For example, workers in the city clerk's office, which gives out birth and death records, dog licenses, and absentee ballots, among many other things, said that with layoffs, "What took four minutes will take 20, or require a trip back the following day." They saw funeral directors, attorneys, and title searchers as potential allies.

The Recreation Department saw their allies as Little League and soccer and lacrosse leagues.

Without a Fire Code Clerk, landlords would run amok regarding regulations on smoke detectors and doors. Loss of the Code Enforcement Officer would increase substandard housing, fire traps, and blight, all of which lower property values.

The Youth and Family Services Department saved at least $10.6 million in incarceration costs last year by diverting 267 juveniles from the criminal justice system.

We instructed members in each department how to interest the press in their work, in order to let the citizenry know what they're getting.

The Children First Norwich program, for example, throws a massive block party every year that brings 2,000 people to local parks. The City Clerk's office provides a free justice of the peace on Valentine's Day—a big day for weddings.

Members were asked to think whom they interact with on a daily basis. The next step is to approach these allies and ask them to contact city council members before the public budget hearings in April, hoping to impact the council beforehand.

A further step is outreach to state legislators. The goal is for the legislature to fully fund grants to Connecticut towns and cities—and to make sure it gets the money to do so.

We are asking to keep educational grants at the same level and to reduce unfunded mandates. We want new ways for municipalities to raise revenue: a real estate transactions tax, a hotel tax, and fair distribution of the Casino Impact Aid Fund (casinos create a huge strain on the budgets of nearby towns).

A member committee planned a breakfast for legislators, with the grateful co-sponsorship of the city administration and school superintendent. We believe we have common ground: the way state aid is allocated is unfair to municipalities.

DO IT BETTER

Our position is that if the goal is to maintain all positions and services, everything should be on the table.

Members have begun scrutinizing city spending habits, partly through info provided through freedom of information requests. They're looking at lost revenue opportunities. Tax abatements and waivers of building permit fees have cost hundreds of thousands of dollars in potential revenue.

Through the lunchtime meetings, strategic planning committee meetings, and our constant focus on the best way to maintain services, creative solutions have started to emerge. The next step will be an alternative budget.

Budgets are about choices. The city came close to losing important services in the last budget cycle. City employees sacrificed to maintain those services. We need to ensure that decisions the city makes do not come at the expense of livability.

It's trickier to end the wage freeze. But we have uncovered unanticipated revenue, and insisting on our wages keeps pressure on the city council not to squander funds and on the city manager to handle wages equitably among departments.

BUILDING A COALITION FROM THE GRASSROOTS TO FIGHT CUTS

by Howard Ryan

New York City is a tough town for teachers and education advocates. Mayor Mike Bloomberg, who controls the public schools, is a corporate operator with a privatization agenda. The city's United Federation of Teachers (UFT), with 108,000 active members, offers meager resistance to budget cuts and the deterioration of teaching conditions.

Yet teachers at Leon Goldstein High School in south Brooklyn have worked to create a coalition that has energized teachers, parents, and other unionists facing cuts. Their experience emphasizes that rank and filers don't have to wait for union officials to lead the charge.

Activists dug deep to connect rank-and-file leaders in several public unions.

The project's initiator, social studies teacher Kit Wainer, said, "Our approach was to try to launch the kind of organizing project the unions should be doing on a much larger scale."

In the latest round of budget cuts, Goldstein lost some of its advanced placement classes and most after-school activity, including tutoring. Worse, the school anticipated losing nearly $300,000 more from the 2012 budget.

In response, the school's teacher, parent, and student leaders formed an ad hoc budget restoration committee, which organized a protest and got 1,000 petition signatures against the cuts.

"We decided we needed to move beyond the school level," Wainer said. The committee reached out to chapter leaders (the union chief at each school) and Parent Association leaders in 80 schools across south Brooklyn.

GOING HORIZONTAL

The outreach wasn't easy, since the committee had few names or contact information. The UFT wasn't officially involved at this point.

Before unions held a big springtime march to Wall Street, a grassroots coalition was already building pressure in neighborhoods against budget cuts.

The Parent Association was no better off. Their district-wide coordinating body was barely functional.

The committee sent a generic letter to each school: "Dear UFT Chapter Leader," or "Dear PA President." The letter invited them to work together against budget cuts and announced a meeting to strategize.

Wainer added that he had a dozen teachers phonebank. "If we didn't have names, we would leave messages for 'the UFT chapter leader,'" he said.

The strategy meeting had a modest turnout, but succeeded in hooking up rank-and-file leaders who had never worked together before. Also, the UFT district representative attended the meeting at Wainer's invitation. The rep backed the new coalition, encouraging chapter leaders to get involved in a protest the union was planning.

The union's official support was significant because the coalition had been launched by an opposition leader. Wainer has long been active with the rank-and-file caucus Teachers for a Just Contract and was its presidential candidate in 2007. TJC remains a sharp critic of

UFT leadership. Why would the UFT authorize its representative to cooperate?

Wainer had deliberately pursued the coalition as a non-oppositional activity. And UFT was happy to see the group target a state senator, a Republican who the union believed was politically vulnerable.

Wainer said the UFT support made a difference: "To be able to put the UFT logo on the flyer really helps. To have the plug coming from the district rep really helps. It puts a stamp of legitimacy."

The district representatives sent flyers to every chapter leader in Brooklyn and talked up the protest at a Brooklyn-wide union meeting. About 200 people attended, picketing outside the office of the state senator, who had voted the wrong way on school cuts.

Younger teachers walked around the crowd with clipboards, collecting contact information and spurring interest in ongoing work against the cuts.

ACROSS THE UNION UNIVERSE

As the group built toward the protest, one teacher, Mike, suggested reaching out to rank and filers in other unions.

Mike's brother works at the power company, so he was invited to address a membership meeting of the power workers' local, which endorsed the action. The activists produced a new leaflet with both union logos. The power union advertised the rally, and sent several members, including top leaders.

After the rally, the coalition broadened its cross-union outreach. The mayor had proposed cutting 20 firehouses (along with 4,200 teachers). Teachers with firefighter friends and family dug for names and numbers of their union delegates and invited them to a follow-up meeting. Two teachers spoke at 20 firehouses, getting hugs and high fives wherever they went.

By this time the UFT and other city unions had launched some actions to protest the cuts. The UFT was a prime builder of a springtime march from City Hall through Wall Street which drew tens of thousands.

The biggest boost to the Brooklyn organizers came in June 2011, when half the student body at Goldstein High staged a walkout to protest the budget cuts. None of the faculty had organized the walkout—even tenured teachers can be fired for doing so.

But student organizers said the teachers' actions had created a buzz among students about what the budget cuts would do to their school. The students had seen the picket lines before school in two earlier protests, and seeing teachers take action helped legitimize protest in their minds.

At the chosen moment, student organizers appeared together to distribute leaflets urging students to walk out. Student marshals kept the protesters walking along the sidewalk.

After an hour, police arrived and threatened to arrest everyone. The organizers led a march back inside, chanting slogans against budget cuts.

The teacher-parent coalition is contemplating two actions. A march could stretch from one facility facing cuts to another, maybe from a transit depot to a firehouse or school.

Another idea is a teach-in on budget cuts and the attacks on unions and communities, targeting high school and community college students but looking for transit workers and firefighters as well.

Electoral work is always a major part of UFT strategy, Wainer says. But he thinks labor "should encourage this kind of bottom-up activity as a way of rebuilding union solidarity and combating budget cuts more effectively."

FIND ALLIES, NOT JUST SUPPORTERS

by Greg Asbed and Lucas Benitez

When you read about building coalitions, it can almost sound easy, like part of a do-it-yourself organizing recipe. You find a chapter titled something like "Building Effective Coalitions," read a few general rules, check out a couple of examples from successful campaigns, and off you go to call churches, community groups, and other like-minded organizations to build a coalition around your campaign.

It's never that easy.

FULL PLATES

The toughest part of building a coalition around your campaign is the fact that it's *your* campaign. In today's world, just about every organization has more than enough on its own plate to keep it busy, much less take on your campaign, too.

And even though some groups, like Interfaith Worker Justice committees or the Student Labor Action Project, exist primarily to support labor or community organizing, their plates are pretty full, too. By no means is it automatic that you can just call and they'll be there when you need them.

So how to bring religious, student, labor, and community forces to bear in your battle?

Allies are people who join your fight for their *own* interests as much or more than yours.

The Coalition of Immokalee Workers grew out of the Immokalee, Florida, farmworker community—one of the poorest, most isolated communities in the country. We have been extremely fortunate when it comes to coalition-building. Over the past several years, our community has benefited immeasurably from a growing alliance of organizations across the country committed to holding major food corporations accountable for human rights violations in the fields where their tomatoes are picked.

Together, we have demanded a food industry that doesn't rely on the endless exploitation of farmworkers.

LESSONS LEARNED

We've learned a few lessons over the past several years that have been key to building the coalition of allies behind our campaigns. We began organizing 15 years ago in Immokalee and for several years we were focused exclusively on directly confronting the local powers of the produce industry, crew leaders and local growers, through community-wide strikes, marches, and hunger strikes.

We didn't even think about building a coalition of allies around our struggle during those years, as our strength and our base was the community itself and our employers had no name or brand in the public eye.

Over time, however, we realized that the industry our members work in didn't end at the farm gate. If it did, no one would ever eat the food our members worked to harvest and pack. Rather, the industry that begins in Immokalee's fields ends on tables across the country and the real power in our industry lies in the companies that sell you the food you put on your table.

The power to force down wages in the fields is in the hands of companies like Publix, McDonald's, and Walmart, and our organizing was going to have to confront those powers if we were to make real change in Immokalee.

So, our first lesson was really internal—we had to identify the forces shaping the conditions we were organizing to change before we could reach out to other organizations for help to take on those larger forces.

While we may not have needed allies to wage our struggle locally, we realized quickly that if we were to take on the $100 billion fast-food industry, with its billions spent every year in advertising, we'd need a few more people on our side. A campaign on the national stage would require a national network of allies.

ALLIES, NOT SUPPORTERS

Once we understood that bigger picture, we made a crucial decision: we were going to set out to find *allies* in our fight, not supporters. What's the difference?

Supporters generally come to your cause as outsiders, motivated by

Allies joined a Coalition of Immokalee Workers march on Publix Supermarkets in Florida.

sympathy or solidarity, but motivated by their feelings about *your* issue. Allies, on the other hand, are people who join your fight for their *own* interests as much or more than yours, people who want to take on your adversary for reasons of their own.

We looked at our potential allies. Young people targeted by the fast-food industry were exploited in their own way as consumers. At major demonstrations in Seattle, Washington, and Miami they had mobilized to fight corporate control of their lives. Joining forces with, and respecting the autonomy of, our student allies was a natural and obvious move.

The same held for our allies from the faith community. Many members of faith-based organizations and churches seek to make decisions in their lives, including their decisions as consumers, based on their faith's vision of justice.

By joining forces with our campaign, those organizations joined a battle that sought to reshape the food industry, an industry central to all our lives, in a way consistent with their own vision for a more just economy.

Finally, we could not build effective coalitions if we ourselves were not strong. The same solid community base from which we began our struggle 15 years ago in the streets of Immokalee is the base from which we lead our campaign at the national level today.

Though we are spearheading a national campaign with many allies, we can never afford to take our eye off the ball right here in Immokalee. The source of our strength and the glue that keeps our diverse allies united is the unquestioned leadership, consciousness, and commitment of the young immigrant workers who pick the tomatoes you eat.

L.A. TEACHERS USE PRIVATIZATION FIGHT TO BUILD COMMUNITY POWER

by Noah Lippe-Klein and Sherlett Newbill

When the Los Angeles school district announced that Dorsey High School was subject to takeover by a corporate charter company, the Dorsey community was ready to fight.

Immediately, a team of teachers, students, and parents distributed 5,000 flyers—starting at our school's enormously well-attended Friday football game and spreading out into the community that weekend. "This is about your child's future," said the flyer, inviting people to a "major community meeting" to "help us come up with our fightback strategy."

A school's anti-privatization struggle depends on community engagement.

Dorsey teachers were ready to fight to save our school because we had already spent several years building our union chapter and community organizing through Progressive Educators for Action (PEAC), an influential rank-and-file caucus in the 40,000-member United Teachers Los Angeles (UTLA).

BRICK BY BRICK

Located in South L.A., Dorsey crowds 1,700 students into a school built to serve 1,000. Fifty-six percent are African-American and 44 percent Latino, and most are poor enough to qualify for free or reduced-price lunches.

Until 2007 the union chapter was inactive: meetings rarely took place and the chapter had no genuine relationship with parents and community members. We decided we needed to get organized.

Sherlett Newbill is a PE teacher, varsity basketball coach, and lead teacher in one of Dorsey's Small Learning Communities. A Dorsey alumnus and lifelong community resident, she has served as a mentor to hundreds of students over the years and formed long-term relationships with parents and community members.

Noah Lippe-Klein is a history teacher who had been doing community organizing with a parent/student/teacher organization called the Coalition for Educational Justice and had contributed to building PEAC.

We knew we had to replace the union chair, but we wanted to do it by building a new leadership layer in the chapter, one with a social justice vision of getting teachers and parents organized.

We sought out potential leaders who believed in the vision and who had roots in the community and the school—a new leadership core that was majority African-American and Latino.

Through lots of meetings at coffee shops and at our homes, we built a consensus for what a bottom-up, activist union chapter should look like.

We won the chapter chair election and formed a steering committee. We asked its members to build relationships with parents, work on teaching conditions and improving instruction, and draw connections between our school's issues and the union's district-wide and statewide actions.

We formed strong relationships with parents and community, leading to a coalition called Dorsey Family United. DFU led a campaign for better funding at Dorsey, aimed at improvements such as smaller class sizes, more counseling staff, and maintenance of bathrooms.

We supported a student-run chapter of the Coalition for Educational Justice (CEJ) on campus, which joined the struggle against dis-

trict-wide cuts. We supported the successful fight against privatization at one of our feeder elementary schools. We fought proudly and militantly against budget cuts and layoffs—which included a PEAC-initiated, UTLA-sponsored civil disobedience to protest layoffs of teachers and counselors.

Over these months, the teachers learned to trust their allies' ability to lead. Students and parents responded to this trust by taking their own initiatives.

For example, after last November's announcement that Dorsey was on the list to be given away to a charter company, CEJ student leaders met with the principal to think through ways to inform every student what it would mean. They created a student-led information campaign including student-made buttons and a Facebook page.

TURNING OUT

Four years of grassroots organizing, community building, and leadership development is paying off now that Dorsey is on the list for potential private takeover.

A community forum drew 250 parents, students, teachers, administrators, and alumni to address the privatization threat facing Dorsey and three other area schools. The turnout came from hundreds of phone calls by teachers to parents.

At the forum, we followed a presentation with break-out sessions—one for each targeted school—where attendees could start discussing actions. The break-out groups were then incorporated into school site organizing committees at each school.

The committee at Dorsey involves 40-50 people who meet every Thursday after school in the Dorsey library. It also includes various Saturday or evening meetings for working parents. The committee is now envisioning the kind of school we want Dorsey to be, after which we will write a plan to submit to the district within the competitive bidding process.

The committee will organize for a strong (if non-binding) community vote supporting its plan. To prevent the school board from giving Dorsey to a charter company, we will use local media, gain the support of longtime civil rights organizations in the community, and prepare for a powerful and massive mobilization. We are campaigning jointly with the other three affected schools in our area.

Even if our plan prevails at the school board, we recognize that neither Dorsey nor the school district has the resources necessary for the visionary school we want. Yet the anti-privatization struggle provides a much-needed opportunity for community engagement and empowerment.

New leaders are emerging every day who are committed to the fight to improve Dorsey and who connect our fight to a much larger agenda for quality public education.

GETTING MEMBERS INVOLVED IN OCCUPY'S NEXT PHASE

by Joe Berry and Helena Worthen

Every steward in North America must have members who are talking about the Occupy movement. Maybe your union has endorsed Occupy officially. Perhaps you have participated in some Occupy action yourself.

Certainly the rapid spread of the movement made many union members optimistic in a way that we haven't been for a long time. The idea that the 99% can actually stand up to the 1% is contagious.

Occupy Wall Street marched against bank foreclosures, and helped a family move back in after they'd been evicted.

How can stewards build on this moment of opportunity to strengthen the union? After all, the issues Occupy has been raising—economic inequality, thievery by the banks, failure of the corporations and rich to pay their share in taxes, increasing unemployment and insecure employment—are the same issues the unions have always fought.

As the encampments have mostly been destroyed across the country, the movement has morphed into thousands of actions pursuing the same general goals. Some places are focusing on protecting residents from foreclosure and evictions, some are holding actions at banks, and some, like Occupy Education or Occupy Post Office, take the Occupy idea back to where people work or need services.

STOPPING FORECLOSURES

In Detroit, a big United Auto Workers local has been sending officers and staffers to help stop foreclosures, in actions carried out by Occupy and other local groups. "We're looking to collaborate with anyone working for social justice," says Local 600 President Bernie Ricke.

The coalitions have stopped two home foreclosures and one of a popular theater that is Occupy's meeting place.

In the most dramatic action, the protesters used cars to block the street near a family's targeted home. A simultaneous delegation to the foreclosing bank resulted in a back-down: the family will be allowed to buy their home for $12,000.

Asked if some members resented the union's working on behalf of non-members, Ricke said, "We can do both. We have a moral responsibility to help people in our community. On the foreclosure issue, there might be a disconnect for people who have their house paid off or aren't underwater, but we just say to them, 'what have all these foreclosures done to the value of your home?' They can see that it does affect them."

Longshore and Warehouse (ILWU) Locals 6, 10, and 13 in California are exploring a program to mobilize their members for community fights.

They're looking to emulate the Service Employees. In the '90s, SEIU locals used their hiring hall dispatcher (who gives out job assignments) to put the word out to members that the hiring hall would be held that day at a site where janitors were picketing.

"Those that didn't get called on for work right away would have the option to join the picket line, and most did," said the ILWU's Peter Olney. "It sure beat the hell out of sitting at the hiring hall playing cards, and it was a great way to build up a culture of solidarity amongst members."

Now the focus is on home defense. Occupy Long Beach hosted a workshop on foreclosures, with ILWU members in attendance, and member participation in actions against home foreclosures in San Francisco and East Oakland has been slowly growing. The key is linking it to challenges facing members' families, Olney said.

Union members in Minneapolis, including activists from AFSCME Local 3800 (university clerical workers) and SEIU Local 26 (building service workers) have participated in several Occupy actions defending homeowners as well.

In November they were successful in keeping Monique White, a North Minneapolis resident, in her home. Now White has opened her home as a base for neighborhood organizing. Two dozen volunteers conduct regular neighborhood canvassing to generate support for White to stay in her home, and to identify and recruit additional homeowners in foreclosure willing to work with occupiers to fight back.

"Unions here have walked the line pretty well between supporting Occupy and not trying to co-opt it," said Nick Espinosa, an activist with Occupy Minnesota.

CULTURE CLASH

Occupy, with its "mic checks" and general assemblies, is culturally a long way from a typical union demonstration where everyone wears the same color T-shirts and leaders speak from a stage.

But the fact that the two cultures are supporting each other is something to celebrate. It's very different from what happened in the anti-Vietnam war movement or even the civil rights movement.

Head to your local Occupy general assembly yourself and see what's happening. Occupiers may be activists, but that doesn't mean they know more than the average American about unions and how the labor movement works. You can have some interesting conversations. Come back and talk about what you see, good and bad.

The exercise of political speech at work, including posting things on bulletin boards, wearing 99% stickers, and encouraging participation in the actions raised by Occupy can both educate members and engage them in the messy optimism of the movement, substituting courage for fear and banking solidarity for the future.

Chapter Eight

STRIKES AND CONTRACT CAMPAIGNS

HOW UE MEMBERS OCCUPIED THEIR PLANT

by Leah Fried

The last day of work at Republic Windows and Doors in Chicago was to be December 5, 2008. But managers soon realized that workers would not go quietly: they had voted to occupy the factory.

Members of United Electrical Workers (UE) Local 1110, they'd made plans to scatter throughout the plant, chain themselves to the machines, and risk arrest. This is the story of how they did it.

The occupation that won workers their back pay and the admiration of union members around the world didn't happen out of the blue. It was the culmination of years of struggle to build a democratic, fighting union able to take on the boss.

LAYING THE FOUNDATION

In early 2004 workers at Republic suffered under a gangster "union" that represented the boss more than the workers. Chicago is one of the last bastions of these old-school outfits that help companies keep workers down.

Unity among the workers, and solidarity from the community, took years of patient effort.

Workers had their wages frozen at $8 an hour for three years and had seen hundreds of their co-workers fired for no good reason. Discrimination, unfair treatment, and low wages were the hallmark of their former union, Novelty and Production Workers Local 16. So workers sought a change.

First they approached several worker centers, which arranged a meeting with UE organizers. Workers were impressed with UE's record of democratic, aggressive unionism. In November 2004 they organized an election, joined UE, and went on to win their best contract ever.

In the contract fight of 2005, workers regularly wore UE buttons and stickers with contract demands. They organized marches to the boss's office, practiced picketing, and voted and publicly vowed to strike if necessary. A contract was won on the eve of the planned strike, with raises of $1.75 immediately and improvements to working conditions and benefits. This struggle set the tone for years to come.

Unity, however, wasn't automatic. Democratic unionism doesn't exist without some growing pains.

Republic workers are a diverse workforce: 80 percent Latino, 20 percent black, and 25 percent women. Hotly contested elections for stewards and officers, intense debate, divisions based on race or gender—all took place in this local.

Leaders had to work hard to build black-brown unity, overcome factionalism, and be willing to lose some debates (such as one over a dues increase) in order to create a local in which all the workers felt ownership.

Some leaders of the occupation had campaigned against each other in elections and each had their own following. But in the end, the workers were able to come together every time they needed to fight the boss.

UE had also been dedicated to building alliances in the community and the labor movement. Years of work to forge links with worker centers, religious groups, community organizations, and immigrants rights organizations laid the base for solidarity.

Rank-and-file members' longstanding participation in solidarity activities, Jobs with Justice, and immigrant rights marches in Chicago helped local leaders get to know UE better. And regular participation in national political action helped lawmakers know UE as well.

PLANNING AHEAD

UE began planning for a possible plant occupation in November, when machinery started disappearing from the plant. Local leaders were prepared for the worst-case scenario.

We bought chains with locks and organized a core group committed to civil disobedience if necessary. We knew it might come down to getting arrested, but workers understood they had to keep the company's assets from leaving the factory.

As workers met again and again to talk over what might happen and organize for a fight, we developed a strategy that focused on Bank of America. The bank, which had just received $25 billion in bailout funds, would decide whether Republic would continue to receive financing.

UE reached out to allies and elected officials to mobilize public pressure on the bank, including a big picket of its offices in Chicago two days before the occupation. Members of Congress, most significantly Representative Luis Gutierrez, pressed the bank to negotiate with the union.

The occupation was launched after the company didn't show up to a meeting with the bank and UE. Workers came to their last day of work on Friday, December 5, and decided unanimously not to leave until their demands were met: vacation pay, 60 days' severance as the law required, and two months' health insurance.

The company was informed of the workers' vote to occupy the factory. They knew they faced more than 200 angry and organized workers who were not about to leave quietly.

Management called the police, but at the same time our longstanding allies mobilized hundreds of supporters, via urgent alerts and phone calls, to come to the plant.

By this time the press had become a steady presence. The idea of the whole world seeing 200 workers dragged out by the cops in front of a supportive crowd rallying outside the factory—it all helped the company decide not to fight the union.

The police left, and the chains stayed in their bags. The workers had taken the plant.

As word of the factory takeover spread, solidarity started pouring in, from unions and community, religious, immigrant rights, and civil rights organizations. The messages visitors left on posters in the plant lobby, the donations, and letters from all over the world were key in strengthening the workers' resolve.

But most important was the unity of the workers, who despite their differences, rose to the occasion and showed incredible strength.

MAKING IT REAL

The day the occupation began the local executive board and stewards organized their co-workers into three shifts, round the clock. UE organizers also took shifts (although those tended to last 20 hours).

Rules were agreed upon and posted in the cafeteria: No alcohol, smoking, or drugs. Non-UE members, unless immediate family, were not allowed onto the factory floor.

A meeting inside during the sit-in.

Committees for welcoming and security at the door, clean-up, food, and patrols to keep the assets safe were staffed in eight-hour shifts. At the beginning of each shift all the workers and organizers would meet to give updates, take volunteers for each committee, and review what would happen that day.

Workers kept busy with rallies and press interviews outside the plant in addition to their committee responsibilities. Children accompanied their parents, doing homework and playing amid the adults' work. Donated food, blankets, and two TVs (one for news, the other for sports) were shared equally by all.

After six long days, the lead committee made up of shop leaders and UE reps came back with a settlement that workers voted enthusiastically to accept. We had won all our demands and then some.

But we know that something beyond jobs or money owed has been won. We have inspired millions to know that the world is what we fight to make it, that we can win.

[Four years later the UE workers would repeat the feat, winning another reprieve for the window factory by re-occupying the plant.]

PREPARING FOR, AND WINNING, A PUBLIC SECTOR STRIKE

by John Braxton and Karen Schermerhorn

A campus union spent months uniting members and making the case in public before hitting the bricks.

Can strikes work for public employee unions in an era when public treasuries are stretched thin? The 1,300 faculty and staff at Community College of Philadelphia answered that question with a clear "yes!" in a two-week strike in 2007.

Bargaining started more than a year before expiration for 200 classified employees (clerks, housekeepers, and other non-teaching staff), 450 full-time faculty, and 650 part-time faculty who form the three separate bargaining units within American Federation of Teachers (AFT) Local 2026. The local has had numerous strikes in its 37-year history, but the most recent one was a decade previous.

The stalwarts who built our local are heading towards retirement, and nearly half of our current membership had been hired since the last strike. Furthermore, different groups of members have somewhat different interests, making it unclear whether we could establish unity, or whether management could exploit the differences to their advantage.

INTEREST-BASED BARGAINING

Early on, the administration proposed that the two sides engage in "interest-based bargaining." Sometimes called mutual gains bargaining or "win-win" bargaining, this approach has both union and management list their interests on particular issues and meet in committees that brainstorm possible solutions to the problems, without initially committing themselves to any particular solution.

The leaders in our local were concerned that interest-based bargaining might lull some members into believing that all issues could be resolved simply through discussion. On the flip side, we thought that some of our members might think that we were needlessly combative if we rejected interest-based bargaining.

As a result, we decided on a two-pronged approach: (1) engage in interest-based bargaining on certain issues that might lend themselves to this approach and (2) mobilize our members in a contract campaign that would build up to a strike if necessary.

OPEN THE BOOKS

Using a new approach, our local hired a leader of another AFT local who led several meetings to help us plan the campaign. This helped us identify goals for our campaign and themes that would help us communicate with our members, our students, and the public.

Knowing that the administration would be asking us to cut our health care coverage, we decided to focus on the fact that the administration had spent hundreds of thousands of dollars on a new branding campaign and hired lots of new administrators, all while raising tuition rapidly, turning away students, and claiming there was no money to give faculty and staff health benefits and decent raises.

We decided to pull one of our experienced rank-and-file members out of half of her classes to coordinate our mobilization campaign. We also hired a seasoned union-side public relations consultant who helped us develop our message.

In December, after members of the administration refused to divulge their salary ranges or how much money they were paying health care consultants, we posted signs and leafleted the campus with the slogan, "Faculty and students open our books every day. Why won't the administration open theirs?"

PRACTICE STRIKE

Although some of the interest-based bargaining committees came up with proposals acceptable to both the union and management, it became increasingly clear that on other issues the administration was intent on dramatically reducing the power of the union. Management wanted not only cutbacks in health care, but also to gut seniority protection for part-time faculty and tenure rights for full-time faculty.

To prepare our members, our students, and the public for the possibility of a strike, we decided to call a "practice strike." We carried our picket signs in front of the college entrances, with the "On Strike" line partially covered by stickers saying "Just Practicing," attracting good media attention.

All of this build-up meant that by the time we decided that negotiations had bogged down, our members were prepared and voted unanimously to strike.

REAL THING

When we hit the bricks, the picket line combination of the mostly blue-collar and pink-collar classified employees with our white-collar faculty was exciting. The chants, songs, line dances, tambourines, and drums were captured on every TV station and area newspaper for two weeks.

Only a tiny number of members crossed the picket line. Student quotes in the press mostly called on the administration to settle the strike in a fair way. Jobs with Justice and the Coalition of Labor Union Women helped out in rallies and on the picket line, connecting the strike to the broader labor movement.

Interestingly, the crisis created by the strike was felt not only by the administration but also by political leaders. Newspaper coverage focused on the important role that the college plays in building an educated workforce that improves the tax base in the city, and the failure of the city government to provide adequate funding.

In the end, a labor-friendly congressman stepped in and arranged for an additional $800,000 to be made available, which was facilitated by our local's connections with AFT Pennsylvania and the AFL-CIO. The victory was only partial, as the administration insisted that the extra money be distributed in the form of bonuses, rather than added to our base pay. Nevertheless, our strike resulted in a settlement that was better than what we had been offered before the strike. Just as important, we had created a new group of rank-and file activists and a new sense of unity for the struggles ahead.

SYMPATHY STRIKES AND THE LAW: IS SOLIDARITY LEGAL?

by Robert M. Schwartz

Q: I work at a company where the production workers and the technicians are in different unions. The techs' contract runs out this year while ours has a year to go. If the techs call a strike, can the production workers respect their picket lines?

A: Possibly. For much of the 20th century crossing another union's picket line was unheard of. When one union went out, workers in other unions and workers at other company locations would often stop work in support. In some cases, whole cities shut down.

Solidarity strikes dropped off after World War II when many unions signed no-strike clauses in return for grievance arbitration. These clauses subject workers to discharge for striking during the contract. Some contracts even expressly bar sympathy strikes. Congress dealt a further blow in 1947 when the Taft-Hartley Act gave employers the right to sue unions for contract violations. In some cases, courts have awarded millions of dollars in damages for illegal strikes.

Teamsters could legally honor US Foods picket lines in 2011 because they won a contract provision that allows it.

Labor law recognizes two exceptions to a ban on sympathy strikes. The first applies if the strike being supported is an "unfair labor practice strike," such as a walkout triggered by the employer's refusal to bargain. If workers honor the picket line of a ULP strike, they have the same status as the strikers they are supporting: they cannot be fired or permanently replaced. (Some contracts close this loophole by inserting language that bars unfair labor practice strikes.)

In some contracts and court jurisdictions, space exists for unions to pull a solidarity strike.

The second exception comes from the National Labor Relations Act itself. This law says that a stoppage to avoid an "abnormally dangerous" working condition is not a strike. Avoiding a picket line may meet this standard if pickets have threatened or assaulted line-crossers.

GENERAL NO-STRIKE CLAUSES

No-strike clauses in some contracts do not expressly bar sympathy strikes. They simply ban strikes, stoppages, and slowdowns for the life of the agreement. Does such general language prohibit workers from respecting picket lines or conducting other forms of sympathy strikes?

For years, the National Labor Relations Board and the courts held that general no-strike clauses did not prohibit sympathy strikes. Judges cited the legal rule that a waiver of a legal right must be "clear and

---

TEAMSTERS DON'T CROSS

Some unions have won the express right to respect picket lines. Article 9 of the Teamsters National Master Freight Agreement says it's not a violation of the agreement if an employee refuses to enter any property involving a primary labor dispute, or refuses to go through or work behind any primary picket line. Very similar language exists in the Teamster agreements with UPS, DHL, and other companies.

Sometimes, however, supervisors will tell drivers to park their trucks outside a picket line. Then a management person from the struck company will come out to drive the truck across or to pick up the package. Still, the delay and hassle for the company means the refusal to cross is a worthwhile show of solidarity. Often truck drivers will call the union hall to find out what to do. If you're planning a strike and want Teamsters to honor it, notify their local unions and their Joint Council in advance, requesting support.

> ## A SYMPATHY STRIKE WITHIN THE SAME LOCAL
>
> University of California public employees planned a strike in 2007—and faced hurdles trying to organize a sympathy strike of their own members. UC workers are under California state law rather than the National Labor Relations Act. Contracts had expired for both service workers such as janitors and groundskeepers and for patient care workers at UC hospitals. Management was bargaining with the patient care workers, which meant they weren't legally allowed to walk. But the service workers were at an impasse—and they called a five-day strike.
>
> The union, AFSCME Local 3299, knew the service workers' strike would be more effective if the patient care workers stayed out, too. But, says UC Davis organizer Amy Hines, "We were not legally allowed to point patient care workers in that direction. Neither were board members."
>
> But the union had a mobilization structure, the Member Action Teams, whose leaders weren't on AFSCME pay. They could promote solidarity strikes instead.
>
> Management threatened to discipline patient care workers, up to termination, who honored the pickets, and that kept the number low. But the union got pro-union state legislators to visit the picket lines, and they told UC not to touch anyone who was on strike or honored a picket line. "UC knew the budget hadn't been passed yet," said Hines, "so maybe they thought about funding at that point." In the end, no patient care sympathy strikers were disciplined.
>
> —Paul Abowd

unmistakable"—or the right was not waived. But in 1985, the Labor Board ruled that a broad no-strike clause should be presumed "as prohibiting all strikes, including sympathy strikes." Unions could overcome the presumption only by proving, through bargaining history, past practice, or other evidence, that the two parties intended to permit sympathy strikes.

The federal Ninth Circuit Court has criticized the 1985 decision. The largest circuit, it covers Alaska, Arizona, California, Hawaii, Idaho, Montana, Nevada, Oregon, and Washington. It said nurses represented by the California Nurses Association could respect the picket lines of an X-ray technicians union represented by the Longshore Workers because a general no-strike clause that does not specify whether sympathy strikes are included or excluded does not constitute "a clear and unmistakable waiver."

WHERE DO YOU STAND?

What does this mean for workers whose contracts contain general no-strike clauses? If you work in a state in the Ninth Circuit, and there is no evidence that your union intended to give up its right to conduct a sympathy strike, you may be able to respect a picket line without risking discharge. (If the strike is economic, however, your job, like that of the strikers you are supporting, can be given to a permanent replacement.)

If you are outside the Ninth Circuit, there is no clear evidence that your employer intended to allow sympathy strikes, and you do not fit one of the exceptions described above, you and your fellow employees can be discharged for respecting a picket line.

A contract that forces workers to cross the picket lines of fellow employees is a symptom of a weak labor movement. Fighting for language that permits sympathy strikes is an essential element to rebuild the power of unions.

STRIKING BACK AGAINST PICKET LINE RETALIATION

by David Cohen

Verizon fired 40 union members in December 2011 for picket-line activity. Aren't members protected in legally sanctioned strikes?

Not always. The courts and the Labor Board have given employers the ability to discipline workers for "picket line misconduct" or "egregious misconduct."

They define misconduct as assaults, property destruction, and extensive blocking of non-strikers, including strikebreakers.

To win, unions must affect business as usual. But unions can prevent firings for strike conduct by mounting massive and disciplined activity that doesn't allow the boss to target a few troublemakers.

Robert Schwartz, in his must-read book, *Strikes, Picketing and Inside Campaigns: A Legal Guide for Unions*, gives examples of how the NLRB has defined misconduct:

- ⇨ Warning a line-crosser, "we know where you live and we're coming to get you"
- ⇨ Throwing rocks or bottles
- ⇨ Banging on a scab's car with a picket sign or spitting on scabs
- ⇨ Placing nails on the road.

The NLRB has extended the concept to include actions or threats that can reasonably be assumed to intimidate or coerce non-strikers from crossing the picket line.

While yelling at scabs and calling them scabs is allowed, coupling that with racial or sexual epithets can get a striker fired.

EDUCATE MEMBERS

Make sure that strikers understand the problem with individually threatening a scab. While it feels good to yell, that's not what wins the strike. Have plenty of chants ready for members to use, and remind them that picket lines are video recorded, so all actions are documented unless a wall of picket signs blocks the camera.

When the strike is effectively disrupting business, there is no need for many of the other actions. They become counterproductive.

Unions can prevent firings for strike conduct by mounting mass actions that don't allow the boss to single anyone out.

If employers restart production with strikebreakers, action must be taken that may violate the law, such as mass picketing. The steward's job is to make sure it is a *mass* activity and that it is disciplined.

That way, any repercussions will be directed at the union, not at a few individuals. The involvement of supporters who aren't part of the union becomes extremely important at this point.

Fifteen weeks into a strike at one small Massachusetts factory, the company advertised to hire strikebreakers. The union mobilized, and hundreds of members from other workplaces and students from a nearby university converged on the picket line. Needless to say it was a wild event.

This continued for several days until the company got an injunction limiting the union to four picketers at the gate. The mass picketing continued—it just moved onto both sides of the road approaching the factory. Picket lines swelled to 500, stopping traffic.

The union was threatened with fines, but claimed it had obeyed the injunction by limiting the pickets at the gate to just four.

After several days the police ordered the factory shut down to restore order. At that point negotiations resumed and a settlement was reached.

DOCUMENT

The union must document threats, name-calling, or aggressive driving by non-strikers. These can be used to show disparate treatment if the employer tries to fire strikers but does not discipline non-strikers for similar conduct.

Keep a log with time, date, names, and exact description of the event.

Most important, the union should include a "no discipline for picket line misconduct" clause in the strike settlement. This will prevent the company from firing people upon their return to work. This, of course, is easier to negotiate if the union settles from a position of strength.

If the union isn't able to get a "no discipline" clause, or the firings take place before the settlement, then the union must grieve and aggressively follow up with information requests. The union needs to show that the employee's actions were not egregious or that the employer is engaging in disparate treatment by singling out some workers.

The union can also pursue a charge with the NLRB, saying the discipline results from legally protected union activity.

MOON OVER MIAMI

Sometimes the union has problems when a member insists on getting into trouble. On one picket line, a member drank heavily despite warnings that this was not allowed. He then mooned the office secretaries, who were not in the union, and was arrested several times for the moonings.

During strike settlement negotiations, the company said it would fire the mooner. The hard fact was that most members didn't want to defend him, because they felt his problems were of his own making. But the union was able to get him reinstated with a suspension.

In similar situations, unions may have to agree to a general "no reprisals" clause but agree that certain cases head to arbitration.

Strikes are tough these days, but we can win by being militant, disciplined, and prepared to protect the picketers in the inevitable settlement.

REVIVING A LOST ART: BUILDING A STRIKE SUPPORT COMMITTEE

by Chris Kutalik

Strike support is crucial to help strikers survive, amplify their message through the community, and pull off actions that the union may not be willing or able to mount.

As in every good contract campaign, strike supporters should begin building as early as possible, before the contract expires and a strike is likely.

But strikers and their supporters have little to no control over how long workers are out walking pickets. An early start can cut the risk of being too little, too late.

While the American Axle Strike Support Committee, in a recent example, was built quickly, stayed organized, and pulled off a major event, it could not overcome the sobering fact that it was organized a week before the 87-day strike in 2008 was over.

The committee, for all its good work, was mostly limited to building support efforts for strikers suffering from the settlement's aftermath.

Organized solidarity efforts can escalate a struggle beyond what the striking union can (or wants to) pull off.

Because major strikes have been infrequent this decade, support committees are often built on an ad hoc, local basis. In many cases, you need to pull together a group of individual activists you can quickly count on for your initial committee meeting.

Do you already work with a group of solidarity-minded union members or other activists in your workplace or community? Pull them in. Know a sympathetic clergy member or community organizer? Bring them along.

If you are lucky enough to be in a city that has an active Jobs with Justice chapter, a central labor council with a "street heat" committee, local unions with a history of supporting other pickets, labor-supporting community coalitions or activist groups, woo representatives from them. Keep in mind that many of these groups are not set up Red Cross-style for instant solidarity relief; pulling them in takes as much patient effort as bringing in individuals.

Strike support efforts in the Detroit area, for instance, often fall back on a loose network of groups such as the Action Coalition of Strikers and Supporters and the Wobbly Kitchen, both of which came out of the Detroit newspaper strike more than a decade ago.

Call and confirm with everyone you reach out to that they are coming to the first meeting.

WORKING WITH STRIKERS

Another important initial step is to get buy-in from the strikers themselves. This may seem like a no-brainer, but messy circumstances can make this tricky. A good goal is to have as many strikers and their family members as you can participating in the committee meetings, with solid lines of communication and trust between strikers and backers.

A good union either will have already marshaled its supporters before the strike or will be eager early on to find and work with supporters.

While the Aircraft Mechanics Fraternal Association had no initial plan for community support in the Northwest Airlines mechanics strike in 2005, the union did reach out to fledgling supporters' committees in the first weeks of the strike in several hub cities.

AMFA Local 5 took it an extra step by forming a solidarity committee of members who went out and walked other unions' pickets, inspiring others in turn to join up with their strike support committee.

Unfortunately, a number of union leaders will be reluctant to work with outsiders or in some cases outright hostile. Sometimes you just need to respectfully convince skeptical or suspicious officers or members that outside support can open another, useful front in their fight.

Think about the best representative from your committee, such as a retired member of the local or a well-known community member, to approach them.

In other cases, where undemocratic or incompetent officers reign and may be antagonistic, look for other local officers or rank-and-file members you can work with—and damn the torpedoes. Tough fights toss up new activists and leaders from the ranks; seek them out.

ONWARD AND UPWARD

Regardless of your starting point, work relentlessly to push your initial support base out broader. Make pitches for your committee at other meetings you attend—and organize others to do the same at theirs.

A public letter of support or a petition can be an organizing tool. As its first task, the American Axle committee wrote a solidarity statement that connected the strike to the broader concerns of the Detroit community.

The statement was used not just to make a symbolic argument for solidarity, but to pull in and publicize a wider range of support by approaching and listing an ever-growing list of key individuals.

The statement was made into thousands of flyers and distributed (make sure to have a union bug on it) to a wide range of organizations.

Use all the media available to get the "y'all come" message out. Write a short press release and send it around to the local press. Set up a simple website on an easy-to-use, free host like www.wordpress.com.

If the strike is national or regional, look outside your city for other committees. A nationally coordinated network, like in the 1992-95 Staley lockout or the 1985-86 Hormel strike, can be a powerful tool.

FORCE MULTIPLIER

Once you have your committee built, figure out where to put your energy. Each strike has its particular needs, and the committee will have to hash out a number of questions. Does the strike look like a winner?

If yes, focus on building broader cross-union and community support and providing logistical support for picket lines. If no, then you may need to also figure out a more dramatic plan of action. Because strikers are shackled by a wide (and increasing) range of legal prohibitions, such as not being able legally to block scabs and deliveries, outside supporters can play an important role in militant actions. Make sure to get buy-in from committee members and strikers about their comfort range.

Solidarity efforts have arcs; a well-thought-out timetable of escalating actions will strengthen the overall effort. Start small with less risky actions such as a community rally and work up the scale.

One example of a middle-range action was a car caravan at the

Detroit airport in which mechanics strike supporters drove round and round the terminal, snarling traffic. Well-supported strikes have upped the ante even further: the Detroit newspaper strike brought out hundreds who blockaded press plant gates over and over again.

Reviving the art of building support committees is a necessary piece in the overall revival of labor's strike weapon.

EVERYTHING YOU WERE AFRAID TO ASK ABOUT LOCKOUTS

by Robert M. Schwartz

Lockouts seem to be everywhere. At Cooper Tire in Ohio, sugar beet plants in North Dakota, the New York City Opera, the National Football League, and Caterpillar's locomotive plant in Ontario, management is using the tactic to try to force outrageous concessions.

A typical scenario: An employer presents a draconian final offer. The union refuses to sign a contract with the new terms, and the employer locks the workers out until they change their minds.

But some unionists see a silver lining. If workers are going to have to take valiant measures to resist an abusive contract, triggering a lockout may put them in a better position than declaring a strike.

A lockout has several advantages over a strike.

A lockout has four advantages over a strike: 1) workers cannot be permanently replaced, 2) they can often collect unemployment benefits, 3) the public will be more sympathetic, and 4) the possibility of getting back pay through NLRB proceedings may put decisive pressure on the employer.

Q. When can an employer declare a lockout?

A. In the early years of the National Labor Relations Act, lockouts were allowed only for "defensive" purposes—to prevent sabotage by the union, for example. But in 1965, the U.S. Supreme Court said an employer could lock out employees "for the sole purpose of bringing economic pressure to bear in support of his legitimate economic position."

An employer can declare a lockout when the contract expires, in reaction to a union's "inside campaign," or when a union offers to return from a strike. An impasse in negotiations is not a prerequisite.

Q. Can an employer hire permanent replacements during a lockout?

A. No. Although an employer can continue operations with temporary employees and workers from other facilities, it cannot hire permanent replacements. All unit employees must be allowed to return to their jobs when the lockout ends.

Q. If a striking union offers to return to work under the terms of the expired contract, and the employer declares a lockout to force the union to agree to its final offer, can permanent replacements who were hired during the strike and union members who crossed the picket line continue working?

A. No. A lockout must include all employees in the bargaining unit as well as any permanent striker replacements. Employees cannot be allowed to work as a reward for scabbing.

Q. Can locked-out employees collect unemployment benefits?

A. In most cases, yes. Forty-one states pay benefits during lockouts. Seven pay benefits if the employer maintains full or nearly full operations. Thirty-four pay benefits even if operations are curtailed.

Q. When is a lockout unlawful?

A. An employer may declare a lockout only to force agreement to a legitimate bargaining position. The commission of unfair labor practices, either before or during the lockout, can make a lockout unlawful.

Q. What kinds of employer ULPs make a lockout unlawful?

A. The most common is declaring a bargaining impasse prematurely (i.e., before the parties have reached a good-faith deadlock on the entire contract).

Others include insistence on a "permissive" subject of bargaining (such as the union withdrawing a lawsuit or an unfair labor practice charge); failure to provide information to the union on a central issue in dispute; allowing line-crossers or permanent replacements to work; hiring new employees on a permanent basis; dealing directly with individual employees; or simply refusing to bargain.

Q. What is the penalty for conducting an unlawful lockout?

A. The usual NLRB remedy is reinstatement of all unit employees, with back pay from the date the employer declared the lockout or from the date it became unlawful.

Q. Can a union ever prevail during a lockout?

A. Yes, if workers picket aggressively, form alliances with other unions, build public pressure, pursue local and national boycott campaigns, and collect unemployment benefits (which the employer will have to pay back to the state fund).

The union should warn that if the NLRB rules in favor of the union's ULP charges, the employer may be liable for an immense amount of back wages.

Even if the union is forced to accept the employer's terms, it should be able to get all its members back to work—a result not often seen following an extended strike.

Teamster art handlers in New York City were locked out by Sotheby's, a high-end auction house.

HOW WE BUILT A CAUCUS AND WON A GREAT CONTRACT

by James Fouts, Scott Ranney, and Chuck Norris-Brown

The bus drivers and mechanics of Teamsters Local 597 were about as disconnected as they could be from our union in 2009. Negotiations with the Chittenden County Transportation Authority in northern Vermont were going on, but no one was seriously involved.

Two rank-and-file bargaining team members saw there was no way members could have a voice in negotiations, so one boycotted the process and one resigned. Members voted down the first tentative agreement, but we ended up with worse language on personal time.

We decided it would not happen again. We contacted Teamsters for a Democratic Union and learned how to set up a communications system and a contract campaign. We began to call ourselves the Sunday Breakfast Club, holding our meetings in restaurants.

Long before the contract expiration, we released our own rank-and-file survey.

With this new caucus formed, we addressed internal organization first. We got elected as stewards, which would put us on the negotiating committee and cut our reliance on leaders of the statewide Teamsters local for information.

We started a newsletter that we disseminated member to member. It took a few tries to get right, but when it was fine-tuned, getting information out to 60 drivers and 10 mechanics took a matter of minutes. We also set up a phone tree with communication captains and continued to hold regular Breakfast Club meetings.

Long before the contract expiration approached in June 2010, we released our own rank-and-file survey to find out what the membership valued and where our priorities were.

Those turned out to be resisting part-time work and tightening up discipline language. Management was using "but not limited to" lan-

guage to discipline members for whatever they wanted and was skipping steps for some and not for others. The survey results established a baseline for our contract campaign and started unifying members.

The union leadership, which had been in office for 20 years, put out a survey a week after we did, which seemed to have about five minutes of thought put into it. They would prove repeatedly to be several steps behind where they should have been. We battled to overcome their complacency and get them on the same page, although they weren't happy about a grassroots group telling them how to do their job.

VOTING NO

Union leaders then agreed to a contract that contained a loophole for unlimited part-time work and didn't address discipline. That rallied the members. The first ratification vote—rejected 37-1—certainly quantified our feelings! The parties went back to the table.

We had decided that if the vote was "no" we would pursue the public option and start building for a strike. If the public and other unions stood behind us, we felt we couldn't lose.

We made arrangements for a strike headquarters. We reached out to labor, college students, and the community. We gave leaflets to our riders and talked with them on the bus and at the station. Student supporters at the University of Vermont—which has a big contract with our employer—got the student senate to pass a resolution.

The Vermont Workers Center, an affiliate of Jobs with Justice, educated its members. At a high-energy rally at Burlington City Hall, the president of the Champlain Valley Central Labor Council and many other members of organized labor spoke out.

Most importantly to the drivers, our passengers spoke out to praise the service we provide and to say they would stand with us. Vermont was looking for a reason to stand behind workers fighting for rights on the job.

When management presented a second offer to our members, the union's letter stressed the contract's economic gains. And no specific contract language was provided. That showed us that leaders weren't listening.

NO AGAIN

We campaigned for a "no" vote, but we didn't need to be all that forceful. The vote was 52-6. Half the bargaining unit showed up to watch the count.

By this time local leaders just wanted it to be over. They set a strike deadline five days away.

We had already started strike preparations. We had created a new phone tree and talked member to member to educate and unify people.

The long months of building solidarity, of reaching out to brothers and sisters in other unions, began to pay off. In the final hours before the strike deadline, management asked us to come back to the table.

After 10 hours of bargaining, a deal was made that treated us with respect. Our discipline language now says simply that members will be disciplined for just cause and progressively.

Members say the Sunday Breakfast Club will live on to support all labor in Vermont. Our own members stood up, and many in labor stood with us.

TAKING A CONTRACT CAMPAIGN PUBLIC

by Carol Lambiase

As town leaders in Wallingford, Connecticut, grudgingly lined up to approve health care benefits for the school district's paraprofessionals, they complained they felt browbeaten into taking their toughest vote ever.

They didn't mean to, but the city officials were acknowledging the effectiveness of a public campaign built by the paraprofessionals before and after their contract expiration in 2008.

The school district's 190 "paras" had never received health benefits. In previous negotiations, the issue had divided the membership, because a majority received health benefits through their spouses and supported larger wage increases instead. But after their union affiliated with the United Electrical Workers (UE), a contract survey revealed that more than half the members rated health insurance the most important issue in upcoming negotiations.

The cost of providing health benefits—expected to run $1 million a year—made it clear that a public campaign would be necessary to build support from local residents and convince the Board of Education.

Over the years the role of school paraprofessionals has

changed dramatically. Paras now provide the frontline support to enable the inclusion of children with special needs in public schools as well as provide individualized attention in reading, math, and science. Paras are overwhelmingly women, and not surprisingly, pay and benefits have not kept up with the leap in responsibilities and expectations.

Marshaling the facts and convincing members to get them into the open proved a winning strategy.

Union leaders first began to gather facts and individual stories about how the lack of health insurance affected members. While the contract didn't expire until June 2008, in the fall of 2007 lunchtime meetings were held at all 13 schools in the district, and paras with no health benefits were asked to talk about what going without meant for them and their families.

For some it meant using their entire paycheck to pay for insurance. For others it meant skipping care or going deeply into debt. Their stories were moving and helped to build support among paras who already had health benefits.

GET THE WORD OUT

The next step was to publicize the stories. In the past negotiations had always taken place behind closed doors, and at first members were reluctant to put themselves before the public. But union leaders kept emphasizing that if we were going to get health benefits, we would have to have a public campaign.

The union contacted two local videographers working with a statewide health care advocacy group, who volunteered to film interviews. As word spread, more and more paras agreed to be interviewed on film.

After 17 interviews were completed, a short video touching on the main points was distributed to all the paras and to local politicians, and went up on YouTube. Paras talked to local newspapers and one of them ran the YouTube link on its front page. The local community news channel aired the video continuously.

By January 2008, the building reps were holding strategy meetings to bring community support to the campaign. A petition was developed and paras began approaching teachers, parents, and local residents. Hardly anyone refused to sign the petition, and paras learned that they had a lot more support than they had thought.

At one strategy meeting, they did a power analysis of the town's elected officials. This identified the key players and which paras knew whom. They decided to hold a public hearing, and brought in the videographers and the local Jobs with Justice chapter, who in turn recruited prominent members of the community to form a panel and hear testimony.

Paras began working to mobilize members to attend and to bring desserts. The hearing was attended by 150 people, far more than had ever attended any local union event. When the panel issued its findings on the need for health insurance, paras delivered them personally to school board members at the next meeting.

Paras continued to circulate petitions in schools, outside supermarkets, and at public events. Members attended Board of Education meetings and approached members outside of meetings.

DON'T GAG NEGOTIATIONS

Negotiations began in May 2008. In the past there had been a gag rule in place during bargaining, but UE does not agree to gag rules, and for the first time, members were invited to sit in during negotiations. There were regular reports back to the membership.

Open negotiations greatly increased members' activity. Members wrote letters to the editor, wore stickers, made signs, and took to the streets, picketing before and after work in downtown Wallingford.

Paras filled the room at a Board of Education meeting in November 2008 and their children spoke during the public comments section of the agenda. Letters from parents were presented. Finally, after six months of negotiations, the Board of Ed made a proposal for phased-in health benefits.

An agreement was overwhelmingly ratified in January 2009, and the benefits began six months later. For the first year the district will pick up 50 percent of the premium, increasing each year til it reaches 80 percent. Despite the downturn in the economy, town leaders voted to fund the contract.

The struggle transformed the local, whose president, Annie MacDonald, reports that members used to ask what they got for their dues.

"Now today, we have members who are willing to actively stand up for their rights and are not afraid to speak out for what they believe in," MacDonald said.

CONTRIBUTORS

Paul Abowd is a former Labor Notes staffer who is now a reporter for the Center for Public Integrity.

Greg Asbed and **Lucas Benitez** work with the Coalition of Immokalee Workers.

Judy Atkins is the former president of United Electrical Workers District 2.

Joe Berry and **Helena Worthen** are retired labor educators.

John Braxton is co-president of AFT Local 2026 in Philadelphia, where **Karen Schermerhorn** is co-president emerita.

Dan Campbell has been a co-chair of Teamsters for a Democratic Union, a union organizer, a business agent, and an assistant to local presidents.

Donna Cartwright is co-president of Pride at Work, the LGBT constituency group in the AFL-CIO, and a longtime activist in the Newspaper Guild-CWA.

David Cohen retired as an International representative for the United Electrical Workers.

Jeff Crosby is president of the North Shore Labor Council in Massachusetts.

Richard de Vries is a union representative for Teamsters Local 705.

James Fouts and **Scott Ranney** are current members of Teamsters Local 597 and Teamsters for a Democratic Union, and **Chuck Norris-Brown** is a retired member.

Bill Franks is a senior steward with Wisconsin Professional Employees Council, AFT-W Local 4848. **Ron Blascoe** (retired) and **Barbara Smith** are stewards from the same local.

Leah Fried is a UE organizer in Chicago.

Ellen David Friedman was an organizer for the National Education Association Vermont for 20 years and is a founder of the Vermont Workers Center.

Chris Garlock is director of the DC Labor FilmFest.

Jon Garlock co-curates the annual Rochester Labor Film Series.

Mischa Gaus is an editor of *Labor Notes*.

William Johnson is a former Labor Notes staffer who is now a teacher in New York.

Peter Knowlton is UE Northeast region president and UE vice president.

Paul Krehbiel was a field representative and organizer with SEIU Local 660 in Los Angeles.

Chris Kutalik is a former Labor Notes staffer who now works with UNITE HERE in Texas.

Carol Lambiase retired as an International representative for the United Electrical Workers.

Nancy Lessin is program coordinator for the United Steelworkers-Tony Mazzocchi Center for Health, Safety and Environmental Education.

Noah Lippe-Klein and **Sherlett Newbill** are members of UTLA. Lippe-Klein is a history teacher who contributed to building the PEAC caucus and CEJ community organization. Newbill is a lead teacher in one of Dorsey's Small Learning Communities.

Matt Luskin is former organizing director of SEIU Healthcare Illinois Indiana and Local 880. He now works with the Chicago Teachers Union.

Dan Lutz is a former organizer for Teamsters for a Democratic Union who now works for the New York State Nurses Association.

Jerry Mead-Lucero is the host and producer of Labor Express Radio in Chicago.

Paul Ortiz is associate professor of history and director of the Samuel Proctor Oral History Program at the University of Florida. He is a member of United Faculty of Florida (NEA/AFT).

Guillermo Perez is past president of the Albany/Capital District LCLAA and is now a labor educator and member of USW Local 3657.

Clark Peters is a grievance handler for 1199NE/SEIU.

Charley Richardson is a labor educator and former director of the Labor Extension Program at the University of Massachusetts-Lowell.

Julie Robert is the former grievance committee chair, and **Helen Ho** the former secretary, of the Graduate Employees Organization at the University of Michigan.

Randy Robinson is political economist for the Ontario Public Service Employees Union at its head office in Toronto.

Hetty Rosenstein is the New Jersey state director for CWA.

Howard Ryan is a former Labor Notes staffer who is now a writer and organizer on teachers' issues.

Robert M. Schwartz is a union labor lawyer and the author of several labor law guides.

Tom Smith is an organizer and former president of United Campus Workers-Communications Workers of America, Local 3865 in Tennessee.

Tiffany Ten Eyck is a former Labor Notes staffer who now works with UNITE HERE in Boston.

Young Workers United is a multi-racial San Francisco organization of young and immigrant workers.